CANNABIS INDICA

The Essential Guide to the World's Finest Marijuana Strains

Edited by S. T. Oner
With an introduction
by Greg Green

Volume

1

GREEN CANDY PRESS

Cannabis Indica: The Essential Guide to the World's Finest Marijuana Strains

Published by Green Candy Press

San Francisco, CA

Copyright © 2011 Green Candy Press

ISBN 978-1-931160-81-0

Photographs © Advanced Seeds, AKVC Collective, Allele Seeds Research, Alphakronik Genes, Alpine Seeds, Apothecary Genetics, ASG Seeds, Autofem Seeds, Big Buddha Seeds, Blimburn Seeds, Bomba Seeds, Bonguru Beans, Breedbay.co.uk, Breeder Stitch, Buddha Seeds, CannaBioGen, Ch9 Female Seeds, Chronic Daydreamer, D. Calloway, David Strange, Delta 9 Labs, Dinafem Seeds, DJ Short and JD Short family and friends, DNA Genetics, Dr. Atomic Seedbank, Dr. Canem & Company, Dr. Greenthumb Seeds, Dready Bob, Dready Seeds, Dutch Passion, Dutchman, Elevatorman, Emerald Triangle Seed Company, Eva Female Seeds, Finest Medicinal Seeds, Flying Dutchmen, Fusion Seeds, Gage Green Genetics, Gean Pool, Genetics Gone Madd, Giorgio Alvarezzo, Gnomes, Green Born Identity, Green House Seed Co., Green Lantern Seeds featuring Inkognyto, Green Life Seeds, Grubbycup Seeds by Grubbycup Stash, Hero Seeds, High Bred Seeds by The Joint Doctor, Holy Smoke Seeds, HortiLab Seeds, Irie Vibe Seeds, Jeffman, Kannabia Seeds, Karma Genetics, Karmaceuticals LLC., Kaya, Kingdom Organic Seeds, Kiwi Seeds, Kushman Massive Seed Company, Kyle Kushman, M.G.M. Genetics, Magus Genetics, Mandala Seeds, Master Thai Seeds, MG Images, Ministry of Cannabis, Motarebel, Mr. Alkaline, Mr. Nice Seeds, Muppet Seeds, No Mercy Supply, North of Seeds, Northstone Organics, Ocanabis, OGA Seeds, Original Seeds, Original Sensible Seed Co., OtherSide Farms, Paradise Seeds, Peak Seeds, Pistils, poor white farmer, Positronic Seeds, PureBred Growers, Random00, Red Star Farms, Reggae Seeds, Reserva Privada, Resin Seeds, Riot Seeds, Royal Queen Seeds, RYKA Imaging, Sagarmatha Seeds, Sannie's Seeds, Sativa Tim, Secret Garden Seeds (SGS), Secret Valley Seeds, Seedism Seeds, Seedsman Seeds, Sensi Seeds, Serious Seeds, Shiloh Massive, Short Stuff Seeds, Sinsemilla Street, SinSemillaWorks!, Soma Seeds, South Bay Ray, Spliff Seeds, Stoney Girl Gardens, Subcool, Supreme Beans, Sweet Seeds, T.E., Taylor'd Genetics, Team Green Avengers, TH Seeds, The Blazing Pistileros, The Bulldog Seeds, The Rev, Trichome Pharm, Tropical Seeds Co., Ultimate Seeds, Unknown East Coast Grower, Useless, Vulkania Seeds, Weed World, Whish Seeds, White Label Seeds, World of Seeds, and Zenseeds.

Printed in China by Oceanic Graphic Printing

Sometimes Massively Distributed by P.G.W.

Dedication by S.T. Oner

"I don't care if I fall as long as someone else picks up my gun and keeps on shooting."
— Ernesto "Che" Guevara

As always, I dedicate this book to the fine people at NORML and everyone who has fought against the unjust war on this incredible plant. Now more than ever, the drug law revolution is in sight, and the above quote from one of the 20th century's most inspirational figures should serve as encouragement for us all. Though some may have fallen – the wonderful and very much missed Jack Herer coming immediately to mind – the rest of us must battle on. Education is our weapon and eventually, our war will be won.

I almost feel like the most insignificant part of this wonderful project; the smallest of cogs in a vast and expansive machine that's been working for hundreds of years. My greatest thanks go to Mother Nature herself, for giving rise to this plant that has changed innumerable people's lives for the better.

My most heartfelt thanks also go to the fantastic breeders and seed companies whose work appears between these pages. This book features breeders from the USA, Canada, Holland, Britain, Spain, France, Germany, Switzerland, South Africa, Russia, Australia, Ukraine, New Zealand, and Denmark, and quite a few other countries which cannot be listed due to certain draconic laws against this most holy of plants.

There are some contributors who wish to remain anonymous, but who deserve recognition and respect nonetheless, as does everyone on the online forums, especially the people at Breedbay.co.uk, thcfarmer.com and icmag.com.

Finally I must thank the growers, breeders and writers who inspired me to learn more about this incredible plant; Ed Rosenthal, Jason King, Danny Danko, Mel Thomas, Mel Frank, Greg Green, and Jorge Cervantes are some big ones, and of course the aforementioned Jack Herer, may he rest in peace. These guys are true trailblazers and their tireless efforts set me on my first steps on this wonderful journey. I feel that Cannabis Indica Vol. 1 is a true representation of the variety of cannabis genetics in existence today, and were it not for the hard work and effort of everyone featured in it, it would not exist at all. For this, I say thank you.

Contents

Preface

A Trip With Indica

Just by picking up this book, you are playing a small but important role in the global cannabis community.

Whether you're a grower, a breeder, a daily smoker, an occasional toker, a medical user, an activist, a connoisseur, a horticulturalist, a coffeeshop owner or the kingpin of a growing empire, you are reading this book for one reason and one reason only: you love cannabis!

I wrote it for the same reason.

This book is much more than a few pages of information about the strains that you smoke on a daily basis. This book is the result of months of tireless research, tracking down growers, writing emails, calling nonexistent phone numbers, hunting down breeders from places I'd never even heard of, and digging through years of folklore and rumor to get to the truth about strains we know and love as well as newcomers to the scene. It's the result of years, and sometimes decades, of passion and hard work on the part of the breeders, who dedicate their lives to not only growing this most sought-after of plants (in many cases risking unwarranted jail time and massive federal charges) but also to taking the best of the cannabis plant and making it even better. This book may not have a central narrative but the breeders are the true heroes of the story; they are the nuclear physicists of the movement, pushing their own limits and those of their plants, without whom we'd still be stuck in the dark ages of cannabis cultivation.

These heroes aren't just the celebrated faces we know, gracing the covers of pot

Preface

magazines and the pages of growing forums the world over; many breeders featured here are unsung heroes of the terrible and costly war on drugs. They might not have thousands of dollars to spend on industrial grow rooms or a staff of 20 to produce a new and exciting variety, but they do have more tenacity and drive than many of us could ever hope for. These breeders take their most precious plants, the ones they've lovingly grown right from seed, and walk them through generations of backcrossing and crossbreeding, choosing the best phenotypes, enhancing the best traits of each and stabilizing them until they have a brand spanking new and original strain to call their own. And if this wasn't enough, they then seed the thing and offer it up to the rest of us. We can never be grateful enough.

In this book, I have tried to include a good representation of every corner of the cannabis community: from the established, world-renowned growers that you've all heard of, such as the formidable Sensi and Green House Seeds; through the pioneers you might not have heard of but whose strains you have definitely smoked, like DJ Short and The Joint Doctor; all the way to the absolute unknowns, who grow just for the sake of growing, because they love what they do, such as Russia's Original Seeds and Sativa Tim from the USA. This book contains indica-dominant strains from every corner of the world to provide a truly global view of the cannabis community as it stands today.

That's not to say, however, that the big hitters in the seed game don't deserve our respect. Dutch Passion, Sagarmatha Seeds and Soma Seeds are all represented here and, indeed, their work in the field of cannabis cultivation has paved the way for many smaller companies and individual breeders as well as influencing and improving global opinion of cannabis as medicine. Some of the best and most stable genetics

available come from the futuristic labs of such companies, and these varieties more often than not form the building blocks from which new strains are created.

As you flip through these pages, you'll notice that some strain names come up time and time again. These are the superstars of the breeding world, the strains that changed the way we grow weed and the way we appreciate it too. The prevalence of the Blue family genetics within this book is a testament to the quality of Canadian breeder DJ Short's Blueberry, a strain that has been around since the 70s. Blueberry has become a legend unto itself, known for its high yields and fruity taste, but most of all for its lavender-colored buds that are so popular on the street that they fetch a higher price than most other varieties. Almost every seed bank now has its own Blue offspring strain, many of which are featured in the following pages, and there are now generations upon generations of plants that can be traced back in one way or another to Grandma Blueberry.

Kush is a name that you will definitely have heard, and I don't know a smoker who doesn't get a gleam of excitement in their eyes when you tell them that you've got a stash from this family, whether it be Garberville Purple Kush, Kamoto Kush, Olivia Kush or any of the myriad of strains that don't even list that heritage in their names but still exhibit the incredibly potent and euphoric high that the Afghani/Pakistani variety is so loved for. Kush is revered as a classic strain – and deservedly so.

And it's not just the elders of the strain world that demand respect. Lowryder, the now infamous plant engineered by the genius Joint Doctor, is one of the more contemporary game-changers and continues to spawn an increasing number of tribute varieties. Using the genetics of cannabis ruderalis, a species that had been formerly overlooked by breeders due to its inability to get you high, the Joint Doctor created a

Preface

hybrid that became the first auto-flowering cannabis strain in the world: a plant that managed its own growth, moving into the flowering stage when it was good and ready rather than when its grower remembered to change its light cycle. This blew the doors off the indoor growing industry – from the biggest companies to the rookie cultivator – because of the ease of growing these plants and the productivity of a Lowryder crop. The auto-flowering market has since exploded. There are whole companies now dedicated to producing auto-flowering cannabis plants and, again, almost every seed bank has an auto-flowering variety of their best strain. It's nothing short of a phenomenon.

There's another recent phenomenon in the growing world that I feel I need to address: the listing of THC percentages. It has become popular in recent years to list a THC rating for strains, with the rationale that this is a great indicator of potency. While the level of THC produced by a plant does dictate how baked the bud will get you, it's actually very difficult to test this and get a definitive result; there are numerous methods of doing so and every one has its drawbacks. Even before the bud gets to the testing stage, however, there are problems with assigning one trait to a whole strain. Imagine that you grow a crop of White Widow, and have it tested at, say, 15% THC. Then imagine that you grow another crop, exactly the same, but you've changed your brand of humidifier and this one has a red 'on' light instead of a green one. You probably wouldn't even notice, but your plants would notice the difference when, in the dark periods, they found themselves bathed in the red glow of the tiny new 'on' button rather than their familiar green friend. Such a minute difference can have a huge impact on the health, vigor and, yes, even the potency of a plant, and a one-size fits-all-approach to rating a strain does not account for this at all.

With this in mind, the percentage of THC listed is still a huge, huge selling point

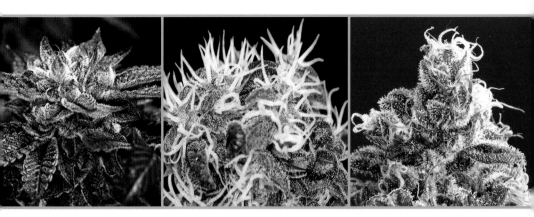

for strains, so the practice of ignoring this difficulty and claiming an absolute potency has become predominant. At the very best, the ratings are unstable and cannot be taken as fact, and in the very worst instances, these levels are straight up invented; it's no coincidence that in the last couple of years the average THC percentage listed has risen from 8 to 10% to 19 to 20%. There hasn't been such a massive leap forward in growing methods that we should expect the average THC level to have almost doubled within a decade!

Whatever your thoughts on the THC debate, it's important to remember that regardless of a strain's potency, there are many other factors that make a good smoke; taste, effects, flavor and smoothness to name just a few. Don't believe everything you read; believe what you smoke!

On that note, I present you with Cannabis Indica: the only strain guide to feature 100 original strains from 100 different breeders from around the world, with high quality full-color photos to match. This is probably the book I'm most proud of, and I'll be forever indebted to the wonderful breeders, seed companies, growers and cannabis lovers featured within these pages whose patience and generosity have made this book the fantastic resource that it is.

No matter what your place is within the cannabis community, whether you're planning to smoke your way through the whole book, flick around and find the strains you love most or have it as a slightly edgy coffee table conversation-starter, I hope that you enjoy it as much as I do.

Introduction

Cannabis Indica: What is it exactly?

By Greg Green

While those of us who regularly puff on a nice stoney joint while strolling through our vast grow rooms may consider indica to be a very good friend, the truth is that an explanation as to what Cannabis indica actually is might be useful for others. And where better to start than the origins of life itself?

In all living things genes are shuffled into diverse combinations through a process of cell division known as meiosis. In sexually reproducing organisms, male and female genes come together like the two sides of a zipper to produce offspring with a mix of the parents' individual characteristics; this occurs because genes are chains of DNA that are transcribed by cell machinery and ultimately translated into proteins that are then assembled into a living thing. This process is ongoing throughout the lives of most organisms and cannabis is no exception.

Cannabis genes are usually expressed in the form of plant morphology and physiology. While genes primarily control plant characteristics, the environment can impact how those genes are expressed; the phenotype is the expressed gene. So, the two things that fundamentally control a plant's phenotype are its genetics and how its genes react to the environment. Cannabis is a plant population that consists of shifting values, and these values are cannabis genes that are expressed as phenotypes.

Shifting values of cannabis genes can be seen when one looks through the pages of this book. Here, there are many obvious differences between plants as well as a lot of common traits. Individual plants can be grouped together based on similarities. Usually plants derived from a parent stock tend to resemble the parents because their

Introduction

genes are similar; in fact, modern genetics uses molecular sequencing to group relationships between living things based on genetic similarities.

Domesticated varieties of cannabis plants are known as strains, and this is the type of grouping that breeders refer to when they talk about their specific stock lines. There are many strains out there, but all can be grouped into three distinct types – or more formally 'species'. The two main types, those that you are most likely to hear about, are Cannabis indica and Cannabis sativa. The third, more enigmatic type, is Cannabis ruderalis.

It is clear that indica and sativa both evolved from a common ancestor. Less clear is which type is genetically closer to that common ancestor, as there is not enough data on this topic. Also, while there is no denying that Cannabis sativa and Cannabis indica do differ, there is some debate as to whether there is sufficient deviation and separation of sativa and indica to support their distinction as different species. On the one hand, they are geographically isolated from each other in the wild, but, like some of Darwin's species of finches on the Galapagos Islands, sativa, indica, and ruderalis can hybridize to produce fertile offspring. We don't have to debate taxonomy here; suffice it to say that knowing the difference between sativa, indica and ruderalis is an absolutely essential criterion for the cannabis cultivator who wishes to interbreed the species.

Let us first address the characteristics of ruderalis. Unlike the other cannabis species it auto-flowers, meaning that it's flowering phase is triggered by plant maturity rather than by the photoperiod. The vast majority of cultivators do not grow ruderalis because it has limited psychoactive properties, though newer hybrid breeds of cannabis have harnessed its auto-flowering trait to great effect. A more popular choice, indica does not auto-flower but is responsive to a photoperiod, as is sativa. The most obvious difference between indica and sativa is average height; indica plants are much shorter than sativa plants, which can be described as 'squat' by comparison. Another distinctive set of features is leaf attributes; indica leaves are short and stubby, much like the overall shape of the plant, while sativa plants tend to have more leaf blades that are narrower and longer, as well as longer internodes or distances between branches. In addition, indica grows much more quickly than sativa and has a more rapid flowering time. It is the combination of these traits that makes indica especially popular with indoor growers. Indica plants are generally more compact because genetically their internodes are much shorter than sativa internodes.

There is no one best way to grow indica plants but, because they grow compactly, their strength is in numbers per square foot. Whether you're working with a basement or closet grow, or a SOG or ScrOG setup, more indica plants can be utilized per square foot than sativa plants.

Indica often appears as a landrace. A landrace is a cultivar that hasn't been particularly domesticated or bred, containing many of its wild counterpart's traits. In truth, while indica has not been influenced much by modern humans, it is being used and cared for and so is not strictly 'wild' either. While some pure indica strains currently used for breeding purposes probably originated as landraces, once a landrace is hybridized it ceases to be a landrace and is on the path toward becoming a domesticated strain because the hybrid population includes domesticated genes.

Knowing all this is essential to a cannabis cultivator, but in order to grasp what truly sets indica apart from the other types, we must understand that cannabis is a truly extraordinary plant not just because of the way it grows, but because of its unique relationship with human beings. The human body actually contains receptors that appear to respond to the cannabinoids contained in cannabis exclusively. The best explanation for this is that, at some point in our evolutionary past, these receptors were used for a specific purpose but that, since then, cannabis has coopted them in exaptation, coevolving with humans to produce a complex symbiotic adaptation.

What sets indica apart is the way in which its cannabinoids interact with these receptors; in other words, the type of high that they induce. Indica plants produce what is known as a couch lock stone as compared with the more cerebral buzz associated with sativas. This means that the effect of an indica smoke is felt predominantly in the body, with stronger strains leaving you unwilling or unable to move from your location, which is likely the couch. In other words, the cannabinoid content in indica-based strains induces a more physical than heady response.

Indica's intensely physical effect and growing traits are at the root of the species' prominence in indoor cultivation over the last 40 years. While the appearance of indica in Western culture is probably a later event than that of sativa, its relative popularity has grown exponentially since the 70s. It appears to have replaced sativa in most indoor grow operations in the late 70s and especially the 80s onwards.

Arguably the most well-known modern indica by reputation is the infamous G-13 or the Hash Plant, but the true indica has to be Afghani#1, which is very popular not only as a standalone indica but as a breeding base for many other indica based hy-

Introduction

brids. If you come across any indica strains, chances are that Afghani#1 genes are in there somewhere. The strain known simply as Afghani has been said to be more Afghan than Afghani#1, and if you are breeding for indica then finding this strain is a good idea. Kush strains are also very popular and similar to Afghani, and these are both major players in the beginners' market. They produce resilient, hardy plants with reliable genetics and results that are usually impressive. Kush and Afghani strains are much admired by breeders, and Skunk x Afghani crosses in particular are very popular. Basically, Afghani can be considered the pioneer of indica plants. Other popular pure indica varieties worth noting are White Russian (Serious Seeds), Sensi Star (Paradise Seeds), Matanuska Tundra (Sagarmatha), Master Kush (White Label), Lowryder (High Bred Seeds), Kong (Holy Smoke Seeds), Deep Purple (Subcool/TGA) and Blueberry (DJ Short).

These days, the trend in breeding indica is to hybridize it to create strains that are known as indica-dominant. Due to the presence of other genetics, usually sativa genes, strains that are indica-dominant or 'mostly indica' tend to be taller than pure indica strains but also bring more of a cerebral high along with the couch lock effect. Because of this, pure indica hybrids that incorporate some sativa traits are extremely popular.

The term 'mostly' used in conjuction with indica has a wide range of meanings but usually, if a strain is labeled mostly indica, it means that more than half of the plant's traits resemble indica. It is normally the type of high and the plant's growth pattern that are noticeably indica; it would be unusual find a strain advertised as mostly indica that dealt a head high instead of a couch lock stone effect.

If you need to determine the species of your cannabis plants, consulting the strain description is also important, as some breeders have been able to create strains with considerable cerebral highs and label them as mostly indica. If the strain is unknown, visual inspection for leaf type and plant size is a good telltale sign. Do not use internode lengths as a way to judge strain type as growing conditions influence these considerably. If you're trying to work out which type of buds you just bought, sampling is also a good (and enjoyable) way to judge whether your stash is indica or sativa. Another indicator may be the size of the bud itself, as sativa colas and bud sites tend to be smaller; however, there are small sites on indica plants too so the size of the bud cannot be used alone to determine type. Simply sampling more sativa and indica can help you determine which type you are looking at, but, again, this will not always be

Introduction

foolproof. The thought of experimenting with all these traits like a 'Pepsi challenge' is, however, quite alluring.

An interesting point about indica and mostly indica strains is the way in which they are named. While there is no true pattern, they tend to have more memorable names than pure indica strains. Black Domina, Maple Leaf, Shiva Shanti, Master Kush, Chronic and Blueberry are all good examples of this. Other popular mostly indica strains include Shiesel (Bonguru Seeds), P-91 (Stoney Girl Gardens), Kushdee (ASG Seeds), Caramel (Poor White Farmer Seeds), Burmese Kush (TH Seeds), Blue Mistic (Royal Queen Seeds), and Adonai Kush (Kushman Massive Seed Co.).

Ultimately, if your goal is to breed indica, I would recommend sticking to the Afghani, Hash Plant and Kush lines to be assured of indica-dominant genetics. Many of these lines do have some sativa influence so be aware that one is rarely ever working with purely indica genetics. However, by selective breeding over generations, most sativa influence can be diminished. Some breeders have opted to create colorful and creative indica-sativa hybrids

Every breeder's goal, regardless of what cannabis variety they're working with, should be to create something that makes an impact. To this end, the most important thing a breeder can do is to keep their strain on the market for as long as possible. Strains come and go, but a lengthy duration will eventually bring a strain into the minds of the cannabis community and keep it there. Many strains that are very popular, and some within these pages, have a 20+ year history with the Western commercial seedbank scene. I believe it is this that offers someone who is interested in breeding indica the best possible way of achieving success. The longer you breed, market, improve and sell that strain, the better your chances of going down into the history books. You should also consider that the person who goes back to Afghanistan to find an even better template for indica genetics, to go in and look at large populations, to find that extra nice plant that is better than all rest would forever been known as an indica maverick. Perhaps that maverick could be you.

CANNABIS
INDICA
The Strains

Adonai Kush

Kyle Kushman and Shiloh Massive are the guys at the centre of the new wave of Earth-friendly styles of cannabis growing and, to this end, produce plant-based nutrients and growing techniques based on 'living systems'. For this strain, breeder Shiloh Massive has crossed his beloved Russian Kush plant with Silvertooth, which itself is a hybrid of Super Silver Haze and Sweet Tooth #3. This offspring has been inbred to the f6 generation and has been fully stabilized.

Adonai Kush has an impressive genetic back list, which makes it a remarkably fun and interesting plant to cultivate. Because of the Super Silver Haze and Sweet Tooth #3 background via Silvertooth, this plant really yields an enormous amount of bud for an indica-dominant. The big buds of Adonai Kush prefer a dryer finishing time to prevent mold from developing. Similarly, because of the high yield and heavy flowers, be sure to stake these plants well, especially if growing outdoors in a windy location. The sturdy Russian Kush genetics provide a lot of toughness and reliability to the plant, so Adonai Kush is very hardy and works great as a commercial grower's strain, or as some delicious head stash.

Expect a very lazy, lethargic stone from Adonai Kush, with a decent dose of the munchies coming on before too long.

Kushman Massive Seeds, bred by Shiloh Massive

Indica-Dominant

Genetics: Silvertooth (Super Silver Haze x Sweet Tooth #3) x Russian Kush

Potency: THC 19%

kushmanveganics.com

Afghani Milk

Afghani Milk is a solid strain stemming from the Ch9 Female Seeds breeding program. Ch9 Vintage 2006, a powerfully bred plant comprised of Afghani, Power Plant and Jack Herer genetics, has been bred to an extremely fast growing Mazar-i-Sharif hybrid that was an underground hit in Holland several years ago. The Northern Afghani genetics really shine through, and the white trichomes common to Mazari plants are definitely visible.

The high resin production of Afghani Milk plants means that they are extremely sticky when in flower, so be careful when handling. The structure is short, and the plant grows quickly, making it ideal for beginners trying out a closet operation for the first time, as well as anyone needing to keep their grow on the down low, literally as well as figuratively. As with any fast-growing plant you should ensure that the growth doesn't run away with itself; make sure the plants don't succumb to pest problems in the hidden depths of the lower branches or grow too close to your lights. Keep the lights in your grown room at least 8 to 10 inches away from the tips of your plants, or they can burn. These plants do grow well under LEDs, so if you're wanting to have a foray into the newer lighting world, and want to avoid the problems of high electricity bills and light burn on your crop, try these under an LED set up. This does involve a high initial cost for the lights themselves, but if you're interested in moving forward in your growing techniques it could be worthwhile. The sight of the resin on these plants underneath an LED light is enough to make any stoner smile, so try it if you get the chance.

Ch9 Female Seeds, Europe

Indica-Dominant

Genetics: Ch9 Vintage 2006 x Mazar-i-Sharif

Potency: THC 18-22%

ch9femaleseeds.com

If the buds become too heavy for the branches to properly support them, you can use stakes or netting to secure them, which is within reach of decent light. Expect a yield of about 65 to 70 grams if you operate on a vegetative state of 35 to 45 days, and a flowering time of 7 weeks.

A very tangy, hashy taste and smell erupts from this resinous beauty. Depending on the amount smoked, and your own state before you smoke it, the effect can be near-narcotic in its high which is fast working and lingering, though couch lock doesn't creep up. I've heard a lot of medical patients comment on this plant's ability to relieve stomach pain and alleviate spasms from multiple sclerosis. Medical patients can smoke this plant safely and be productive in their daily lives as the high is not overly heavy or lethargic but rather a head buzz with some mildly energetic cerebral effects.

Afghanica

The award for Best Company Name has to go to Holland's The Flying Dutchmen, as they've managed to reference nautical folklore and find not only a nod to their home country but also a neat reference to 'flying' high. Such a name is perfect for this great company that has been in business since 1998 in Amsterdam. The quality of the 'true breeding' strains that it took as its genetic foundation means that the Flying Dutchmen are very highly thought of in the scene, and rightly so. With their original strain Afghanica, the company has taken the famously hardy Afghan indica and introduced it to Skunk, one of the most famous cannabis strains of all time. Considering that 'The Pure' strain, also from the Flying Dutchmen, is said to actually be Skunk #1, the plant could very well be cannabis royalty!

The typical rugged, sturdy constitution of the Afghani plant is not lost in this mix, which should be among the easiest available strains to grow. If your budget and space is low, this is a great single plant to have in a small soil-based closet grow, but she is also a fantastic choice for both SOG and ScOG set ups. If you are looking to move into organic or veganics (plant-based) growing, perhaps choosing this strain for your first chemical-free crop would be a good move; it's hardy enough to act as a test subject while still producing and not wasting your time. Though you should not let the plant's apparent invincibility lead to complacency, it will be resistant to some of the usual problems, especially stress and a few of the less intense diseases. Whatever your set up, pests could still be a major issue, so be sure to check all over your short, dense plants whenever you can. The Skunk genes come through in the form of increased growing speed and a greater yield than you would get from the Afghani alone, and the buds will be tightly packed and very solid. Remember, this plant is very problem-free, but you still need a well-ventilated grow room because mold is every grower's worst nightmare.

Flying Dutchmen, Holland

Indica-Dominant

Genetics: Afghani x Skunk

Potency: THC 18%

flyingdutchmen.com

The classic Afghani heritage is clearly evident in this strain. You will recognize and love the thick, greasy but sweet taste almost instantly. For a heavy smoke, though, it's relatively smooth, and tends towards a taste of hash if used with a vaporizer. The high won't hit you instantly, but when it does, you'll know about it. The Skunk influence in this hybrid gives a strong, mellow high that you will feel throughout your whole body, and might leave you feeling a lot heavier than you usually do!

Afgoo

The USA-based Northstone Organics is a medical cannabis farm that also grows organic fresh produce and employs sustainable practices; proof of their genuine care for both the quality of their cannabis plants and their impact on the environment. For the fantastically-named Afgoo, they've mated an Afghani Kush with a Maui Haze, a sativa-dominant plant from the shores of Hawaii, and come up with an offspring that's quite the pleasant grow and an even better smoke.

Afgoo plants display the usual small stature of indica influence and very wide leaves, with some enormous fan leaves during vegetation. The leaf-to-calyx ratio can be high on some plants, but after harvest the trim is great for hash making and production of medical edibles. They have a high tolerance for nutrients and will thank you for a good feed with a growth spurt, but also you need to also make sure that they have sufficient access to good light sources.

This is a very sedative strain, which calms and relaxes both the body and the mind. The smoke can be a bit coughey, but is worth it just for the sweet, piney, warm taste alone. It works predominantly on the body, can put all but the strongest everyday users down for a good night's sleep if the buds were left longer before harvesting, and gives a mildly euphoric haze.

Northstone Organics, USA

Indica-Dominant

Genetics: Afghani Kush x Maui Haze

Potency: THC 20%

northstoneorganics.com

Atomic Northern Lights

Atomic Northern Lights is Canadian breeder Dr. Atomic's version of the classic Northern Lights #5. He has preserved this celebrated plant through a selective breeding process, keeping it mostly indica but with a 14 to 20% sativa component that provides the lingering and prolonged high. Originally, Northern Lights #5 was bred for vigorous growth, great yield and long lasting effects. Dr. Atomic has created a connoisseur grower and breeder's dream plant by preserving and improving upon these classic characteristics.

Atomic Northern Lights is an indoor strain that grows as a short, bushy plant, making it ideal for closet grows. The buds tend to have a frosted look because of the copious trichomes, and when this plant is happy its fan leaves will curl upwards, as in the photo. The plant has a short and stocky structure, which means it is easy to grow indoors and remain discreet about things. Flowering time for Atomic Northern Lights is about 8 weeks and yield is up to 125 grams per plant.

Dr. Atomic Seeds, Canada

Indica-Dominant

Potency: THC 17%

dratomicseedbank.com

The prolonged, intense high that accompanies smoking Atomic Northern Lights is fantastic. Dr. Atomic has over 40 years of experience as a cannabis breeder and enthusiast, and this sweet, smooth smoking plant is ample evidence of his mastery of the breeder's craft.

Auto Bud

Auto Bud by Autofem Seeds is a cross breed from a Lowryder x Big Bud male, which provides the auto-flowering genetics, and a Hindustani female known for her beautiful colors and extremely dense yields. This plant is heavily influenced by William's Wonder (from the Lowryder genetics) and subsequently produces very dense, resinous buds. By utilizing Lowryder and Big Bud genetics, Autofem Seeds has very cleverly created a plant with the positive characteristics of three of the greatest indicas ever created: Big Bud, William's Wonder, and, of course, Northern Lights #2.

This plant is an auto-flowering variety, again due to the Lowryder genetics, and can be planted and harvested in a 60 to 70 day cycle with no change of lighting. Indoor growers can expect a harvest of 55 grams if they use 12 to 20 liter pots, 600-watt lamps and put the plants under 20 hours of light per day. This strain has been used industrially to great effect, but is also great for small, manageable closet growing.

Auto Bud nugs give a very enjoyable indica stone with a lot of Big Bud flavors and

Autofem Seeds, Spain

Indica-Dominant

Genetics: Lowryder x Big Bud / Hindustani

autofem.com

a strawberry smell. Potency is high, and the stone comprises a good degree of couch lock and some surprising but welcome cerebral activity that sneaks in halfway through. These two play off against each other for a fantastic experience all round.

Auto White Domina

Kannabia, one of the first Spanish seed banks, has been breeding for a number of years and currently offers a variety of original seeds, including many auto-flowering strains. To create this Auto White Domina, the team at Kannabia crossed the requisite ruderalis with a White version of the selectively-bred Black Domina, which itself has Afghani, Canadian Ortega and Northern Lights heritage with a big dose of Hash genetics. Black Domina has become a very popular strain since its inception, and its White sister should do likewise due to its straightforward and reliable growth.

Kannabia Seeds, Spain

Indica-Dominant

Genetics: Ruderalis x
Black Domina

Potency: THC 20%

kannabia.es

A tall ruderalis parent brings an unlikely height to this plant, which thrives particularly well in a SOG set up. Despite having a heavy indica dominance, Auto White Domina will look different to all the others in your set up and should be treated accordingly. A big central cola is surrounded by lateral branches and will take up as much space as you give it. While indoors, the plant will only normally reach around 3 feet in height, if you have the space to grow her outside you'll find yourself face to face with a 6.5 foot monster. If you're planning to clone your White Domina, this can be done 3 weeks from seed, and it might be a good idea to top the plants, making them bushier and with more sites to clone from. A breeder's tip with regard to cloning is to take cuts 20 minutes after watering. Within 7 weeks these plants can be harvested, with a slightly higher rate of production if you can leave them a little longer. Either way you'll get a good amount of resin and a lot of pointed, compact buds. Even an indoor grow will yield around 400 grams per square yard of grow space. The plant is mold resistant and doesn't usually become the victim of the typical weed diseases. If you're located in a Mediterranean climate try an outdoor grow, which should be ready to go around the start of September thanks to the enhanced growth speed that the bigger root expansion allows for. In either circumstance, pruning the lower branches will concentrate the plant's energies into making that huge central bud even bigger.

You'll recognize the Afghan taste straight away, but the hint of citrus might surprise you. They call this strain an "almost devastator": the high is somewhat incapacitating, though bearable and even pleasant if your immediate plans don't involve a lot of moving around or operating heavy machinery.

Babylonia Fruit

Vulkania Seeds is a popular Spanish seed company based in the Canary Islands. Their Babylonia Fruit is an indica-dominant hybrid coming from a Nepalese landrace plant bred with African and Asian strains to create a hybrid renowned for its potency, yield and outstanding flavor. Cannabis enthusiasts have long known about the incredible genetic potential of Nepalese ganja, and Babylonia Fruit is a perfect example.

These plants are incredibly small and have minimal branching. This makes them not only ideal for an indoor grow if you're tight on space, but means they will flourish especially well in a SOG set up. Though they can be grown anywhere, indoors is their optimal environment and, with maturation at around 7 weeks, you can expect flowering to occur between 55 and 65 days from germination. This makes Babylonia Fruit a great choice for those short on time as well as space. The ease of growing this plant also means that even a beginner would have difficulty ruining a crop. However, if you choose not to use a SOG technique, be sure to leave your plant in the vegetative stage for a fair amount of time to allow for maximum growth. Even a simple organic soil grow can be suitable for these plants and, with the right organic nutrients, they will grow perfectly and look utterly beautiful. Be extra sure to inspect for pest problems throughout the whole of your grow time, as nasty little critters such as aphids can take hold of and ruin your whole crop if you are not vigilant. If you do find any of these pests, there are myriad options to help you get rid of them. As ever, an ounce of prevention is worth a pound of cure. The plants will never grow tall but they will grow wide and bushy, and it is then that harvest is optimized and your patience pays off. If you choose to grow outside, the extra space to stretch out will do them well and the increased room for roots will definitely help their vigor.

Vulkania Seeds, Spain

Indica-Dominant

Genetics: Nepalese Landrace

Potency: THC 16%

vulkaniaseeds.com

These buds may smell as sweet as sugar and even fruity when growing, but don't let this fool you into thinking that this is an easy smoke for the newly initiated. The resulting high from Babylonia Fruit is almost narcotic and surprising in its intensity. Medical marijuana users find this a great strain to help ease chronic pain and anxiety and to induce sleep in those who've been suffering from insomnia, making it popular amongst that community. Of course, its effects are also much appreciated by the recreational user and every true stoner will love the heavy and long-lasting hit of this one, so roll up a J, lean back and enjoy!

Big Buddha Cheese

This Cheese from Big Buddha Seeds is a unique strain that was, until recently, only available as a clone. Cheese originated in the late 80s as one unique female phenotype from Skunk #1 seeds grown somewhere in the Chiltern Hills. This plant produced huge buds and had an incredible cheddar-like odor, and was cloned to become Cheese. Big Buddha bred this UK Cheese backcross with a pure Afghani male plant to create Big Buddha Cheese, one of the most popular strains in the UK.

Big Buddha spent two years selectively backcrossing this plant in order to isolate specific beloved Cheese traits, and now Big Buddha Cheese retains its mother's old school taste and its Afghani father's sturdiness and excellent yields. The flowering time should be 7 to 9 weeks indoors, and you can look to harvest at the end of October outdoors. Because of the high yield, additional support is often necessary, so be sure to stake your plants well in advance of flowering. You will need very good air filtration in your grow room because the aroma is so pungent that it can draw unnecessary attention to your garden.

Big Buddha Seeds, UK

Indica-Dominant

Genetics: Skunk #1 x Afghani

Potency: THC 19%

bigbuddhaseeds.com

The high is very uplifting with no ceiling, and offers a clear, long lasting buzz. Big Buddha Cheese smells very unique, with a pungent, old school aroma that reminds many of some very dank cheese. Expect a solid and fruity taste that leaves you wanting more!

Bigger Pine x Bubble Gum

The Original Sensible Seed company, now based in Spain, has been supplying growing equipment and seeds since the early 90s. A favorite early strain, Bigger Pine x Bubble Gum comprises Colombian sativa, Afghan indica and Jamaican genetics to create a phenomenal plant. The Bubble Gum genetics bring stability and a sweet aroma to these plants and were bred with Bigger Pine, one of the Original Sensible Seed's best-bred plants. Bigger Pine was created from inbred lines of Big Bud and Super Skunk and was chosen for breeding due to its high yield and potency.

**The Original Sensible
Seed Co., Spain**

Indica-Dominant

Genetics: Bigger Pine x
Bubble Gum

Potency: THC 18%

original-ssc.com

These plants are short and bushy, with little spread and a strong structure, and you'll see the influence of the Bigger Pine line in the resinous, pine-cone-shaped buds. The uniformity of your garden will speak volumes about the quality and stability of both parent strains, and if you feed them well and give them lots of light, you'll be rewarded with an immense harvest.

During the curing process the sweetness of the buds will become even more apparent, and if you can wait to taste them, you'll find that a bowl of Bigger Pine x Bubble Gum is both delicious and highly effective.

Blue Donkey Dick

Denver's Karmaceuticals LLC are a cannabis collective with over 110 varieties on their shelves as well as every sort of marijuana-related paraphernalia you could care to think of. We can hardly accuse them of being crude with Blue Donkey Dick, as the name more or less writes itself; its parents are DJ Short's superstrain Blueberry and the brilliant indica-heavy hybrid Donkey Dick from Mighty Mite Seeds. Donkey Dick is interesting as it comes from Vancouver Island originally and is meant for outdoor growing, which is a relatively rare combination on the seed market.

Karmaceuticals LLC, USA

Indica-Dominant

Genetics: Blueberry x Donkey Dick

Potency: THC 17%

facebook.com/karmaceuticals

Donkey Dick is so called for the enormous size of its colas, and this trait is one that has passed down to its Blue offspring. As Blueberry too is known to be a large producer, you can expect a heavy yield from this plant, and one that shares the beauty of the rest of the Blue family, with the purple and blue tints being enhanced by cold temperatures. The plant is very rigid, making it fairly hard to train, but this shouldn't be necessary, as the ruggedness of the plant means that it is able to hold its own weight well. As this strain is well-suited for commercial grows, you should be aware of having enough water and light available to ensure that your harvest will be as profitable as possible as well as of the highest quality. Also be sure to amend the soil before you plant these guys outside, as making sure that you have a good quality soil base will make a world of difference to the growing potential of your crop. If you're growing in the U.S. midwest, this particularly applies to you, because if you're within 10 miles of a river basin the soil will probably be too alkaline and will need something like elemental sulfur or sphagnum peat added to it. As organic grows are purported to enhance the pot's flavor and potency, you could also aim to bring out the very best of this strain's Blue traits by staying chemical-free throughout its growth, if you so wish.

The cured buds of your Blue Donkey Dick plants should be purple in hue and fairly dense. Like its parents, this plant gives an uplifting and positive high along with a fruity smoke that is also a little skunky. This high is extremely long-lasting, so you should only need a few tokes to carry you through the whole night.

Blue Fruit

Dinafem Seeds of Spain has been in the business for almost a decade and in that time has risen to be one of the country's largest seed banks. Their fantastic Blue Fruit strain can be traced back to the mountains of Oregon, with a family tree that includes a purple Mexican, a Thai sativa plant and a particularly high-yielding variety of DJ Short's fantastic Blueberry.

Most Blue Fruit plants are vigorous in growth and may need to be trained or controlled if grown in environments where less space is available, such as indoor set ups or smaller greenhouses. Thanks to the sativa influence, they grow taller than some indica hybrids. It's better to keep the light levels down with this strain, as too much light can stress the plants and cause mutation. As with all Blue strains, colder environments will bring out the delightful blue / purple coloring on the leaves, which compliments the sweet berry taste of this plant perfectly. Your plant will look good enough to eat!

There's no need to go that far though, as the intense and affecting red berry taste of the smoke will be more than enough, lingering as it does on the palate for a long while. As you slide into a psychoactive but calming body and head high, your senses will be going wild, as if you've just eaten a particularly delicious summer berry pie, laced with a very mild hallucinogenic.

Dinafem Seeds, Spain

Indica-Dominant

Genetics: Mexican Purple x Thai x Afghani (Blueberry)

Potency: THC 12-19%

dinafem.org

Blue Mistic

After numerous years growing in the Netherlands, the team behind Royal Queen Seeds decided that the time had come to exercise 20 years' worth of knowledge and produce their own varieties of cannabis that were suitable for all growers, from the absolute beginner to the connoisseur breeder. Since inception, Royal Queen Seeds has won many accolades for its products and Blue Mistic is one of the company's most enigmatic strains. Though both its name and growing pattern suggest that DJ Short's famous Blueberry strain might be found somewhere in its family tree, we can only be sure that its roots lie in the fantastic surroundings of the California hills.

As with most indica-dominant hybrids, Blue Mistic is a compact plant that doesn't need a lot of space to grow to its potential. It makes a fantastic indoor plant, but will also thrive outdoors in most climates, though its favorite environment is one similar to that of its native Northern Cali. Indoors or in greenhouses, Blue Mistic can grow a little larger than other indicas, but should never grow beyond 5 feet, making it suitable for a variety of growing situations. They do, however, tend to prefer growing in small groups of similar plants, and seem to encourage each other in the growing process!

Royal Queen Seeds, Holland

Indica-Dominant

Potency: THC 20%

royalqueenseeds.com

These hardy plants will finish in just over 9 weeks, but the most exciting part of the growing process will come a few weeks before that. Half way through their flowering cycle, the flowers will start to show a stunning blue hue, beginning fairly pale and moving through to a deeper, more sensual tone when harvest nears. The fabulous-looking buds will grow denser and more resinous right before your eyes, and such is the beauty of the plant that you'll barely even notice how much bud she's carrying. A good harvest should give you about 450 grams of dried bud, which is a superb rate of production for such a small plant. She also has the added bonus of barely giving off any aromas in the flowering stage, which negates the need for excessive venting and protects you from the noses of any snitch neighbors.

The buds of all Blue strains enjoy a longer-than-average curing time to really enhance their already fantastic flavor and smell, so if you can keep your hands off your stash you'll be rewarded well in the end. Fruity and sweet, the smoke is light and smooth but carries with it a knock out stone that will leave you feeling like you've been run over with a padded furry blue truck. And I mean that in the best possible way.

Blue North Special

North of Seeds is quickly gaining a very solid reputation in the competitive Spanish seed market. Operating out of the northwest of the Iberian Peninsula, this company was the first medical seed bank established in that area, and the team goes to great lengths with the care of their seeds. Typical to all 'Blue' strains, Blue North Special is a mostly-indica plant that shares the parentage of eminent breeder DJ Short's Afghani Blueberry, but also has in its heritage Beast, a strain which is popular throughout Spain.

Blue North Special can be grown both indoors and outdoors, and thanks to its mildew-resistant properties, it can flourish happily in either environment without too much trouble. If you choose to grow indoors and use a 12 on/12 off light cycle, you can expect flowering to occur at around the 50 to 60 day mark with about 400 grams per square yard being harvested. If a bigger yield is your main concern, then growing this strain outdoors may be a good option, as the yield can be boosted by up to 100 grams when grown outside. However, if you choose to go outdoor, pests can some-

North of Seeds, Spain

Indica-Dominant

Genetics: Blue x Beast

Potency: THC 14-18%

northofseeds.com

times be a problem, from the usual aphids and ladybug visitors to any animals native to your area, including nosy neighbors and dope thieves. If you can keep all these at bay, perhaps with an arsenal of organic or chemical pesticides and strange behavior that makes people voluntarily stay away from your property, expect to harvest around mid-October. This plant displays its Blue family traits in its density and stout shape and in its red, purple and, of course, blue hues that not only make it an enjoyable plant to grow, but also beautiful to behold! As always, because of the Blue family's Afghani roots, this plant likes dry conditions and is great for hash-making. It is a true blue, meaning that it is blue-colored no matter what the weather, but, again as with many cannabis plants, it changes color in colder temperatures. This means that if you like to manipulate your plant colors to make your garden more gorgeous and to give your dope more bag appeal, give it a shot and lower grow room temperature during the last few weeks of flowering!

Once harvested, the bud has a very strong smell of berries and when you roll up your first joint, you'll notice that the sweetness of the smoke lingers pleasantly on your palate. Much like parent strain Blueberry, this strain packs a long-lasting high with a very positive spin, great for socializing and watching a movie that would otherwise suck. A delicious smoke for sure, and the accompanying euphoria makes for an in-spirational experience.

Blue Rhino

Positronics is a well-respected seed company that operates out of Spain. It produces a variety of fantastic strains, including the formidable Blue Rhino, a great cross between the ever popular indica classic Blueberry and White Rhino, a strain that is said to be almost narcotic in its high. These were bred with the intent of creating a sort of 'super strain' exhibiting all the qualities that a grower could want. To ensure that only the best genes were used, Positronics used an original Blue female from British Columbia famed for its sensory traits, as well as a high quality Rhino hybrid of Afghan, Brazilian and Indian ancestry.

As such, Blue Rhino plants have a huge central cola, massive leaves, and an aroma that is pure indica. It needs a lot of space to grow, whether that means a good-sized pot indoors or a nice bit of space in a greenhouse, but to really let this plant stretch its legs and fulfill its promising potential, it needs to be grown outdoors. With the White Rhino mother it can make a great choice for an outdoor commercial grow,

Positronic Seeds, Spain

Indica-Dominant

Genetics: Blueberry x White Rhino

Potency: THC 16%

positronicseeds.com

but as ever, keep your eye on security at all times. These plants won't grow very tall, as they are mostly indica, and won't produce many leaves, meaning the buds will be nice and dank. The branches, however, are very dense, so don't be worried about the lack of space between the nodes as it has enough strength to hold the big buds it will produce. If you're really paranoid about it, you can use stakes to give an additional bit of support to your heavily-laden girls, but this shouldn't really be necessary. Don't be tempted to harvest early or you'll miss the best part of the flowering stage – your buds will puff up in size and density right around the 9 week mark, increasing your yield substantially. The extra time is also said to give a more mature and layered taste to the harvested buds.

Though the size and strength of your plants are testament to the lengthy genetic selection process that the breeders embarked on, only when you light up your first joint will you feel the impact of such specialized choices of parent plant. The Blue family mother is present in the blueberry and gooseberry aroma and taste, and the Rhino father contributes the heavy body feeling and the woody hints. For the first hour you'll get a pleasant buzz, which then slides into a longer lazy feeling. It can be a bit scratchy if smoked through a bong but the effects will be even more evident. Don't plan to be doing much after this smoke.

Blueberry

DJ Short's Blueberry is possibly the most celebrated indica strain on the planet. Legends abound about this plant, and for good reason. Blueberry has been around since the late 70s and is known as a large producer of dense bud, as well as being father to a hell of a lot of Blue offspring strains. The fantastic Blueberry genetics can be found in hundreds of commercially available strains, many of which have become as popular as their parent strain, making Blueberry the Bob Marley of the weed world.

Blueberry plants have a little more stretch than many indica plants and can reach a medium-tall height with long side branches. Yield is great because all of these branches produce sticky, trichome-laden buds sporting medium to large calyxes, and it can be grown indoors or outdoors. Once harvested, Blueberry bud can be stored much longer than most strains, and enjoys a long curing process, so feel free to keep it stashed for a while.

Once your impatience has you reaching for the storage jar you'll find bud with red, purple, and blue hues that have turned lavender in the curing process. The aroma and taste is a fruity reminder of blueberries, and the high is pleasantly euphoric and long-lasting. The stone is so potent that even the most well-seasoned of stoners will get high when they smoke Blueberry, no matter what their tolerance for high grade bud.

DJ Short, Canada

Indica-Dominant

Genetics: Blueberry Line

Potency: THC 16-24%

legendsseeds.com

greatcanadianseeds.com

Blueberry Headband

As the name suggests, this hybrid, with 75% indica content, is a cross between the classic indica strain, Blueberry, and Headband, known to some as Sour Kush. This fusion is a product of California's Emerald Triangle Seeds, a company that specializes in revamping traditional cannabis strains. The Emerald Triangle of the name refers to the Mendocino, Humboldt and Trinity counties in California, an area that has been popular with growers and cannabis connoisseurs for the last 50 years. They have undoubtedly chosen well for this strain in terms of genetics; Blueberry is well known for its beautiful blue hues, which it has passed on to its offspring, and Headband counts Sour Diesel, OG Kush and, of course, the legendary ChemDawg amongst its ancestors.

Both parent plants are large producers, which can sometimes mean, in addition to a plentiful harvest, a huge plant that can only realistically be grown outdoors. Headband in particular is well known for its furious outward growth that makes it 'leggy' and particularly horrendous to grow inside. However, Emerald Triangle combats this by using the strong indica presence of Blueberry to slim the hybrid down. The result is that Blueberry Headband plants can actually be grown quite happily in an indoor grow room and even a well-tended closet garden. The lankiness of its parent strain does mean that the branches may struggle under their own weight when it comes to the flowering stage, even with the strengthening influence of the indica genes, so it may be necessary to use stakes to help support the branches. Just keep an eye out for any drooping near the biggest flowers. If you are growing outside, let these guys grow to their full potential and you'll have a gorgeous garden just before harvest. It is interesting to note that the street value of this weed is relatively high, due to strong demand for blue bud.

Emerald Triangle Seeds, USA

Indica-Dominant

Genetics: Blueberry x Headband

Potency: THC 15-20%

emeraldtriangleseeds.co.uk

Headband is especially well-suited for medical marijuana users as the stone is not overpowering, leaving you able to go about your daily life, and it controls nausea and anxiety well. The high of Blueberry is both euphoric and very long-lasting so, as you would guess, crossing the two produces a smoke which is both energetic and apt to leave you ludicrously happy and in fits of giggles. It also is a great pain-reliever and calms the smoker. The taste is unmistakably Blueberry, but with a light lemon scent from the sativa-dominant Headband. Be sure to savor the flavor, scent, and experience of this great West Coast plant!

Blush

Canada's Whish Seeds are just starting to become more recognized, thanks to strains such as Blush, which was released in 2005 and encompasses both Afghani and Thai genetics. To create the strain Whish crossed the rare and mysterious Berlin with Dutch Passion's Blue Moonshine, a Blueberry offspring with a rich gene pool.

Blush grows best in colder climates, and its Blue traits are enhanced even further by this kind of temperature, so in a colder set up not only will you get the most out of this strain but you'll also have a good-looking crop. It isn't, however, a good choice for SOG, and, being a grassroots sort of plant, favors soil and organic feeding over hydro and excessive chemical nutrients. Powdery mildew should be easily kept at bay, but spider mites are a fan of this plant, so be sure to check for any evidence that they have taken hold. Blush is a good strain to breed from and will yield up to 60 grams indoors.

Blush is a down-to-earth kind of plant and the blue/purple bud has an earthy, natural and almost floral taste when smoked. The high, too, is very chilled; mellow and relaxing with the ability to induce sleep.

Whish Seeds, Canada

Indica-Dominant

Genetics: Blue Moonshine x Berlin (Afghani x Thai x Afghani)

Potency: THC 16%

whish-seeds.com

BLZ Bud

With BLZ Bud, Holland's Seedism Seeds have created an extremely potent indica-dominant G-13 hybrid. It's very resilient and sturdy, with a potency to die for, thanks to its fantastic parental genetics. Train Wreck is an old school sativa-dominant hybrid strain from Arcata in Humboldt County, California that is known to render smokers completely witless, and Silver Haze is a very potent sativa-dominant hybrid that brings a resin-heavy but uplifting high to smokers worldwide. G-13 is another classic old school strain that brings a lot of structural stability and medicinal properties like appetite stimulation to BLZ Bud.

This plant has very typical indica growth patterns, so expect large fan leaves and very little space between internodes. BLZ Bud is happy to grow in most systems, and maintains the potency and flavor of the sativa-dominant hybrids, but mixes them with the sturdiness of an indica plant. If your plant is single stemmed, expect one large cluster of buds all along the main stem with a few budding side branches.

Seedism Seeds, Holland

Indica-Dominant

Genetics: G-13 x Silver-Haze x Train Wreck

Potency: THC 19%

seedism.com

BLZ Bud smells and tastes sweet, sour and spicy owing to the G-13, Silver Haze and Train Wreck genetics. Initially a hard couch lock high, it then gently changes into a heightened state of euphoria, offering a relaxing sedative buzz.

Buddha's Sister

Buddha's Sister from the celebrated Soma Seeds of Holland was formerly named Soma Skunk V+ but was rebranded to better suit her growth patterns and the sublime high she delivers. Buddha's Sister is a sibling of the tall, lanky Siddhartha, but by crossing the Reclining Buddha with Afghani Hawaiian, Soma has both increased the yield and maintained the sweet taste of the Reclining Buddha plant. Soma's plants prefer organic growing techniques, and are reliable plants for beginners.

The buds are slippery and silky because of the abundance of greasy resin, meaning you need to be careful not to touch your plants too much before harvest. Buddha's Sister makes lots of side branches, so unless you are an experienced grower with time to meet her extensive needs, it is better to grow her as a multi-branch plant instead of in a SOG. A soil set up with good doses of plant-based nutes would also do fine. Buddha's Sister has fluffy, loosely packed buds making it mold resistant, and the multi-branch stature keeps yield high.

Soma Seeds, Holland

Indica-Dominant

Genetics: Reclining Buddha x Afghani Hawaiian

Potency: THC 18%

somaseeds.nl

The flavor is like cherry candy and the smell is quite tart, rather than sweet. The resinous buds and leaves are great for making hash and taste especially good if grown organically. The high is very medicinal and therapeutic and offers a powerful cerebral experience.

Bullshark

If Hollywood ever makes a movie about a cannabis seed company (and with Arnie on the case that might not be too far away) that company will be the Bulldog. It started life as an underground smokers' den, which turned into the first ex-sex-shop coffeeshop in Amsterdam, and now comprises locations in several countries, a hotel, and stacks of branded merchandise – a real 'rags to riches' story. The Bulldog Seeds produces its own strains, such as Bullshark, a hybrid of Green House's Great White Shark and Skunk #5. The award-winning Great White Shark brings Super Skunk, South Indian and Brazilian genetics, which result in great yields and a very strong body stone, while the Skunk family, hailing from the original indica/sativa mix, needs no introduction and brings strength and potency to Bullshark.

A 70/30 indica/sativa mix, Bullshark is a simple and fast strain that's suitable for growers of all different abilities, from the newest cultivator to the most skilled breeder. A double dose of Skunk genetics means that these plants give off the distinctive Skunk aroma, while the indica genetics ensure that they stay short and dense through their whole life span. Fat buds will grow along the main stalk as well as the secondary branches, meaning that towards the end of flowering you may need to give some extra support to the plant by staking or netting. Flowering occurs within 8 weeks, and a square yard of grow space will yield between 600 and 700 grams. Outdoors, if you're growing in the Northern hemisphere, harvest will be around mid-October.

The Bulldog Seeds, Holland

Indica-Dominant

Genetics: Great White Shark x Skunk #5

Potency: THC 17%

bulldogseeds.nl

When you're drying these buds, the outside tends to dry faster than the inside and will appear to be crisping up after only a couple of days. However, the buds will not be properly aired out inside, so resist the temptation and leave them to cure until you're sure that the whole bud is fully dry. If you give in and roll up some wet weed, it won't burn and will leave a bad taste (literally) in your mouth.

A smooth smoke, Bullshark has the strong body effect and skunky sweet taste of its Great White Shark parent. A hint of fruitiness comes through that's not very noticeable while the buds are growing, which is probably thanks to the Great White Shark parentage. The taste lingers delectably on your palate even as the creeping strength of the high takes over your whole body. This heaviness doesn't tend to go away quickly either, so set yourself up for the night with some good entertainment and enjoy the feeling.

Burmese Kush

Netherlands-based TH Seeds have become popular with growers in recent years thanks to their hardy and inventive strains that exhibit very favorable traits. For BuKu, as this variety is affectionately known, they have crossed a Burmese Kush plant with their signature OG Kush family, the Los Angeles strain which has ChemDawg genes as well as Lemon Thai and Hindu Kush heritage. This leaves us with a pretty impressive plant with a fantastic, reliable background.

A speedy plant that flowers in 7 weeks, BuKu has a very low leaf-to-flower ratio making harvest easier and leaving you with more bud for your amount of grow space. It will only grow to about 40 inches, but upon harvest you'll get around 400 grams per square yard. For the commercial grower, this can be a fantastic crop for its ease of growing and, particularly in a hydroponic set up, its amazing yields.

The OG Kush influence is certainly apparent in both the flavor and potency of the smoke, along with a citrus zest that adds something extra. The dried buds are particularly aromatic, and when you're ready to burn one, the smoke is silky and flows well. It's a hard-hitter and is probably going to glue you to your comfy chair, but it also has a nice cerebral lightness that takes away from the heavy feel.

TH Seeds, Holland

Indica-Dominant

Genetics: Burmese Kush x OG Kush

Potency: THC 18%

thseeds.com

Cannaberry

Cannaberry is a 60/40 indica/sativa hybrid project by U.S.-based cannabis research pioneers, Allele Seeds Research. The cross was made using a DNA Genetics Cannalope Haze female, a Sensi Seeds Northern Lights male and a Dutch Passion Blueberry female. This plant has two phenotypes, one that is super sativa head stash, and another (pictured here) that grows much like a sativa, but with slightly fuller buds thanks to the indica influence.

Cannalope Haze is a pure sativa from DNA Genetics that flowers in an incredibly fast 8 weeks. Mixing this with the pure indica indoor-growing Northern Lights from Sensi Seeds resulting creates a very versatile plant that can be grown practically anywhere. The stability and high yield of the Dutch Passion Blueberry means that this plant is a solid all-around performer set to become a big player in the medical cannabis scene.

Cannaberry's taste is super fruity with a subtle hint of cantaloupe helps add complexity to the taste. The effects are clear in the head and very energizing, but also offer a great deal of pain relief and help with spasms and inflammation. Check your dispensary for this great strain!

Allele Seeds Research, USA

Indica-Dominant

Genetics: Cannalope Haze x Northern Lights x Blueberry

Potency: THC 18%

alleleseedsresearch.org

Caramel

Previously known as Candied Chem, with the name changed to avoid confusion with another cross, Caramel comes from the private grow rooms of Poor White Farmer Seeds, a single grower based in the USA known for his fair dealings and honesty about his genetics. Originating in Oregon in May of 2009, this hybrid is the offspring of a 1991 Chemdawg cutting mother and Butterscotch Hawaiian f2 father. This produces a plant that is 80-90% indica. It's difficult to trace its lineage back too far, given the mythology that shrouds its Chemdawg mother, but the Butterscotch Hawaiian has a strong influence. There are many different phenotypes of this strain as yet but each is a joy to grow. When the strain is fully stabilized, it is set to be a formidable contender.

Caramel can grow either indoors or outdoors, but is probably a little happier indoors. You'll see that the plant grows somewhat like its Chemdawg mother, a little viney but not too huge with an average spread of about 1 to 1.5 feet. A SOG set up can take advantage of this trait. The temptation can be to overfeed a Caramel but be sure not to succumb or you'll stunt growth and wreck your crop. Also keep an eye out for the mites that seem to like this plant and will have to be removed at the first sign of infestation. Powdery mildew, on the other hand, will struggle to take hold at all. When harvest time rolls around, which should be up to about 70 days when grown inside, be prepared for a great harvest, and the calyx-to-leaf ratio means that trimming is easy and that harvest, as a whole, is relatively stress-free. Just make sure you don't rub your eyes after trimming – you'll regret it.

Poor White Farmer Seeds, USA

Indica-Dominant

Genetics: Chemdawg 1991 x Butterscotch Hawaiian F2

Potency: THC 17%

Once flowering begins you'll notice a distinct smell of butterscotch in your grow room, with an unusual hint of rubber alongside it. This smoke is not for the inexperienced toker and can be worryingly strong. The high can allegedly bring on a mild panic attack if you are not mentally prepared for the effects, so be sure to be in a comfortable place with good people before you get mashed on this one. The high begins with a tightness around the eyes, spreading to the rest of your face before melting somewhat into the rest of your body, moving to a pretty heavy stone. It leaves you feeling noticeably clear in the head and can set you up for some serious giggles. Also prepare yourself for some serious munchies – possibly brought on as much from the mouth-watering butterscotch smell as by the weed itself!

Clockwork Orange

Riot Seeds is a seed company from the US, and the home of the fantastic and enigmatic Clockwork Orange. Its predecessor, from which it got its name, was either the result of a crazy mountain growers's colchicine project or a mutant bag seed find, depending on who you're listening to or what day of the week it is. What we do know is that this was then bred with a G13/Black Widow hybrid from Mr. Nice Seeds to recreate the original mutation while keeping the hard-hitting potency.

If your set up is aeroponic or hydroponic, this strain has the potential to do really well for you, though it also grows great in soil. Bear in mind that a SOG set up isn't advisable as the plants grow giant leaves that necessitate a lot of space. An insider grow tip is to raise these plants organically for the full flavor and potency explosion.

You'll see where the name originally came from when you hold a dried orange/gold bud in your hand, and if you can get over its gorgeous good looks, you can enjoy a very different woody, earthy taste. You should be ready for a massive stone, however, as this strain can be overwhelming if you're unprepared. A very introspective high with therapeutic qualities, it can also leave you with unusable body parts for a short time, which is fun in the right situation! Just don't toke before an athletics competition.

Riot Seeds, USA

Indica-Dominant

Genetics: Clockwork Orange S1 x G13 Black Widow

Potency: THC 21%

riotseeds.nl

COG

COG by Kingdom Organic Seeds is affectionately known by those who love her as COGzilla in reference to her insatiable appetite for root space, water, light and food, as well as her insane growth rates. COG is a cross between head breeder The Rev's Cinderella 99 line and an old Santa Cruz outdoor favorite that is known as OG Kush but actually resembles an OG Kush / White Widow hybrid.

This plant is, as mentioned above, a super-hog for root space, light, water and food. She prefers to grow in the ground but can also be grown indoors if you build a hefty container mix and use larger containers than normal. This plant finishes in 8 to 9 weeks and grows very quickly, giving a decent yield. Her branches have been known to snap from the weight of her buds, so make sure you are ready to use stakes to give the plant extra support if necessary.

COG is a great plant that smells powerfully of grape Kool-Aid and hashish. Smokers love the hard hitting narcotic high because it is soothing and relaxing without making people too sleepy to do anything. COG is known to give users demonic red eyes and acts as a very effective appetite stimulant for medical users.

Kingdom Organic Seeds by The Rev, USA

Indica-Dominant

Genetics: Cinderella 99 x OG Kush/White Widow

Potency: THC 19-21%

trichomekings.net

Cogollon Powell

Dr. Canem & Company Seeds is a breeder's collective that has been operating since 1998, out of Spain, where they breed excellent cannabis strains and raise Bull Terriers. Cogollon Powell (named after a certain US general) is one of their most interesting strains because of the intriguing blend of Big Bud and Afghani genetics. This high-yielding trait has been maintained by Dr. Canem and his crew, and the injection of Afghani genetics has added some excellent drought-resistance and flavor to the plant.

This plant is almost industrial in its bud production, especially outdoors, so be sure to stake your plants well in advance of flowering. Indoor growers should set up rotating fans to encourage stronger stalks and good ventilation for the copious buds. Another option is to bounce the young stalks between two fingers gently once or twice a day for half a minute or so to mimic the effect of wind on the young plant – this encourages stronger and thicker stalk growth, which will come in handy when the heavy buds appear.

Smokers lucky enough to get hold of this strain should expect a very smooth, pleasant smoke that leaves you feeling overwhelmingly happy. Like all good indicas, the high will last a solid four hours. Dr. Canem & Company are enthusiastic outdoor growers, producing some of the most delicious and natural ganja you've ever tasted!

Dr. Canem & Company, Spain

Indica-Dominant

Genetics: Big Bud x Afghan

Potency: THC 17-20%

Cream Caramel Auto

Spain's Sweet Seeds, as the name might suggest, specializes in producing cannabis strains that are sweet, aromatic and tasty. The company has built a very good name for itself due to their careful quality assurance methods and excellent germination rates. The company is also notable for selling seeds in groups of 3, 5 or 10, which is good news for rookie growers wanting to test out their set up or for those who want some variation in their grow room but don't have the room for 100 different plants. Cream Caramel Auto is a result of crossing Sweet Seeds' best auto-flowering plant with Cream Caramel, which itself is an interesting hybrid of East Indian BlueBlack, Maple Leaf Indica and the famous White Rhino, created with the intention of exploiting the vigor of hybrids and bringing uniformity to the offspring.

Cream Caramel Auto plants are perfect for indoor growing, as their East Indian heritage keeps them fairly small and dense, with a large central bud. Unlike some auto variations, this plant not only shares the looks of its mother but also the behavior, with the exception that it tends to rush through the vegetative stage, and the auto-flowering process cuts total grow time down to around 70 to 75 days from seed to harvest. As with all auto strains, you need to be very much aware of the size of the plant in relation to the size of the pot it is in, and ensure that you transplant into a bigger container as soon as necessary. These plants will begin to flower between 20 and 30 days no matter what their size, so if their growth is stunted by a lack of room for the roots to grow, your final harvest will suffer as a result. Near to harvest time the plants will emit an earthy aroma and the buds will be literally covered in sticky resin, which is great for any grower to see. However, this does mean that you must be careful not to touch your eyes or face when you're chopping and to wear gloves to avoid an unpleasantly strong contact high. This might sound fun if you've already had a joint or two, but it isn't.

Sweet Seeds, Spain

Indica-Dominant

Genetics: East Indian BlueBlack x Maple Leaf Indica x White Rhino

Potency: THC 19%

sweetseeds.es

You can be sure that sparking up a Cream Caramel Auto bud will bring you a myriad of flavorsome sensations. The dried bud has a lovely oregano-like smell and the taste of molasses and caramel comes through distinctly upon further inspection. This strain also delivers a knock-out punch of a high: a breathtaking space-out stoned sensation, plus a near dissociative body feeling that must be experienced to be believed. Not for the faint of heart!

Deep Purple

Deep Purple by Subcool is an indica-dominant cross between his Purple Urkle and Querkle strains. Deep Purple was designed to lock down more of the Urkle dominant traits and bring out the musty grape taste that Purple Urkle is famous for. Deep Purple produces a wide range of female plants and not all of them actually produce colors; however, the females that do produce colors are highly prized by connoisseur growers and many consider them to be among the very best indica strains around.

Like many indicas, Deep Purple is a short, stocky plant that exhibits fairly slow upward growth. She offers a medium yield and can be grown indoors or outdoors, depending on your preference. Subcool recommends that growers give Deep Purple a long vegetative stage and carefully trim some of the shade leaves to allow light to shine on the flowers. These plants are quite hardy and can handle beginner errors, but experts love them because of the complex genetics and the challenges involved in growing purple strains. Expect a harvest window of 50 to 60 days and a decent, tasty yield.

PHOTOS BY OCANABIS

Subcool and Team Green Avengers, USA

Indica-Dominant

Genetics: Purple Urkle x Querkle

Potency: THC 17-18%

tgagenetics.com

Deep Purple has an uplifting, musty grape smell to it that gives this bud some great bag appeal, and exhibits the soft purple coloration that comes with it. Expect a taste like grape snow cones that offers a strong, uplifting high, known to be an excellent anti-depressant and mood lifter.

Deimos

Deimos is a hybrid from Spain's celebrated Buddha Seeds. This indica-dominant plant represents the culmination of years of breeding over seven generations of Northern Lights and Ruderalis plants in order to obtain an auto-flowering plant with the classic Northern Lights features that you know and love. Expect a great indoor or outdoor plant with a hardy, resilient nature and good lateral branching with a respectable yield.

Deimos grows vigorously upwards and outwards creating a bushy and dense yet compact plant. Careful breeding has led to a high yielding auto-flowering plant with lots of lateral branches that can yield buds as large as the central cola. Growers love this plant because of its discreet size – it ranges from 2.5 to 3 feet in height, making it suitable for secret indoor and outdoor grows.

Growers who enjoy continuous harvest set ups will love Deimos as it is a fast growing plant that can go from seed to bud in two months and supply smokers with a constant supply of ganja. To get the fastest results from your Deimos plant, you should grow in less than eighteen hours of light per day from start to finish. Try planting two and then waiting a few weeks and planting two more, and then repeating this process as the plants mature. This way you'll have a continuous harvest period, meaning you'll always have good pot waiting for you at home!

Buddha Seeds, Spain

Indica-Dominant

Genetics: Northern Lights x Ruderalis

Potency: THC 17%

buddhaseedbank.com

An important aspect to be aware of when growing Deimos is that, because it is such a vigorous plant, it likes to have a light nutrient feed after it has been growing for two weeks, but keep it very light as you don't want to burn the young plant. Once flowering begins put the plants on a flowering nutrient regime for weeks four through six. Remember that you should flush your plant for two weeks prior to harvest to remove the taste of fertilizers from your bud, so just be careful to schedule your feeding and flushing to accommodate the fast finishing time of an auto-flowering strain. Auto-flowering strains tend to like root-stimulating nutrients like Phosphorus, but again, be sure to flush before harvest as it makes the bud taste cleaner, and only buy fertilizers that are "food safe" and suitable for tomatoes or another vegetable-type plant.

Deimos is a great plant to smoke because of its devastating potency and its classic sweet and tangy taste. Many people enjoy this plant to help them relax and think things over slowly, and others like to smoke Deimos and watch a movie with friends.

Devil

Holland's Mr. Nice Seedbank comprises three breeders, most notably Shantibaba and Howard Marks. Devil is a Shantibaba cross-breed of Afghani indica and an Afghan/Skunk which favors outdoor grows but also fairs well in a greenhouse set up.

If your grow room is an indoor one, a good hydroponic system will help you get the most out of Devil. Whichever set up you choose to use, don't fret if your Devil plant shows slow growth at the start, as it needs to establish a decent root ball be-

Mr. Nice Seeds, Holland

Indica-Dominant

Genetics: Afghan x

Afghan/Skunk

Potency: THC 18%

mrnice.nl

fore it spreads its green wings. Once the vigor picks up it's a great plant for new growers, as it is easy to cultivate, will end up wider than it is tall and doesn't emit too much odor. Indoors you can expect flowering any time after 8 weeks, or by the start of October in the Northern Hemisphere.

The devilish traits come in the sour smoke and the bud's ability to send you on a journey through your own mind, which of course could be torturous for those who are less than pure of heart. For us pleasant toking folk, though, comes a magical high which feels like therapy, and eases you into a relaxed mental state.

Double Dutch

Magus Genetics from the Netherlands has been involved in breeding and growing for over 20 years and, in this time, has secured access to some fantastic genetics. This includes a pre-2000 female Chronic, the product of a Skunk/Northern Lights, AK-47 and another Northern Lights plant. This plant was crossed with Magus Genetics' own aptly-named Warlock male, which has its roots in Skunk and Afghani indica strains. Double Dutch has a lot of indica genetics in her gene pool, but the sativa influences are also evident, especially when you go to harvest your giant, super dense buds.

Magus Genetics, Holland

Indica-Dominant

Genetics: Warlock x pre-2000 Chronic

Potency: THC 18%

magusgenetics.com

Double Dutch grows with big green leaves, a robust stature and very sturdy stems. Despite its hardiness, this plant must be staked due to the weight of the sativa-like buds, which will grow to epic proportions in the flowering stage and, if exposed to a lot of light, will even start to look like massive popcorn balls. Remember, when staking you are always advised to start early because once the flowering stage begins the weight gets packed on ridiculously fast. You don't want to risk damaging the stalk or branches because you staked your plants a day late. Similarly, because the buds are very heavy, indoor grow rooms need to be very well ventilated to avoid the risk of mold developing.

These crops will grow well in bio, coco and especially well in hydro grow systems, and both topping and training can bring out great results. Towards the end of flowering, 1000 watts of light can be suitable to optimize bud formation. Placing your lights effectively is enormously important because Double Dutch loves direct sunlight. Be sure to plan your grow room's organization in advance to ensure that each and every plant gets enough light, and if they do, should expect a great harvest of about 4 to 5 ounces per plant.

Smoking these popcorn nugs will give you a strong and layered buzz, affecting both mind and body. You may recognize the taste as being somewhat similar to Cheese, but with a more aromatic aftertaste and lingering flavor. The Double Dutch aroma is a lovely wildflower scent with a fruity bouquet. The high comes on after a slight delay, and is complex and strong, as well as skunky with a very noticeable but clear impact on the head with some heavy body effects, too. Smokers should be aware that the buzz can last from two to four hours depending on the smoker's tolerance level.

Double Fun

Holland's No Mercy Supply are serious about providing the best quality cannabis strains and growing supplies to the world. Double Fun is their best outdoor plant, but being a 75/25 indica/sativa hybrid, its size and stature means it grows happily indoors, too. Double Fun was a cross between Citral, a 1993 KC Brains clone not to be confused with the variety available later on the market, and the legendary but enigmatic Dr. Weedman, an early-flowering variety whose genetic history is all but unknown.

Double Fun is resistant to both mold and fungi, and is a highly stable strain with just one phenotype available. Industrial growers love a Double Fun crop's uniformity, because it means they can grow fields and fields of Double Fun and accurately estimate their yield. These results will include fat, extremely resin-covered nugs coated with white hairs that will be ready for harvest around 60 days from seed. Whether you're growing indoors or out, you can expect a harvest of around 350 to 500 grams per square yard of grow space.

No Mercy Supply, Holland

Indica-Dominant

Genetics: Citral x Dr. Weedman

Potency: THC 16%

nomercy.nl

actiontekhd.com

The buds of this plant are distinctly lemon-smelling, but have a sweet citrusy smoke that dances around the taste buds. The strong psychoactive effect, however, gains more fans than the flavor and will leave you remembering this delightful smoke for a long while.

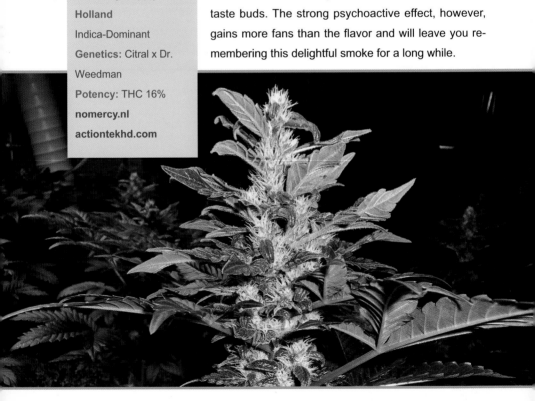

Double Kush

The Double Kush plant from Holland's excellent Delta 9 Labs is a cross between T.H. Seeds' Kushage and Delta 9 Labs' pure Afghan male. The Kushage was a phenotype that leaned towards its Kush side and had more orange colored hairs than pink. The male plant was a heavy Afghani indica that helps make Double Kush a big bud producer.

Double Kush likes to be grown in a SOG set up and the yield increases if grown hydroponically. Growers can give their plant a heavy feeding of around EC 2 at the

highest point during the feed cycle, but be sure to flush before harvest. Double Kush tends to grow more like a bush and doesn't stretch, so it can easily be maintained at less than 3 feet in height. The outdoor flowering time is at the end of October and the indoor time is 9 to 10 weeks. The yield is approximately 400 to 500 grams per square yard of grow space.

Recreational and medical users enjoy the fruity taste and smell of Double Kush. Similarly, people worldwide enjoy the heady indica buzz with its uplifting tones, and medical users especially appreciate the high pain and ocular relief this plant can offer, due to its high CBD content.

Delta 9 Labs, Holland

Indica-Dominant

Genetics: Kushage x Afghan Kush

Potency: THC 16%

delta9labs.com

Dready Berry

Dready Seeds is the breeding project of Weed World columnist and celebrated cannabis connoisseur Dready Bob, and his strains are fast gaining popularity worldwide. One of the most popular is Dready Berry, an F1 Blueberry and White Widow hybrid. This is quite the gene pool to swim in, with the acclaimed Blueberry from DJ Short being a breeder's favorite and White Widow having dominated the scene since its introduction to the market in 1995, most notably in the coffee shops of Amsterdam. The plethora of Blueberry strains available these days are testament to the quality and popularity of these genetics and just mention White Widow to any stoner to understand that this mix is one to pay attention to.

Adaptable to both indoor and outdoor grows, Dready Berry goes mad when grown outside and can end up growing as much as ten feet high. It is quite the formidable looking plant as its blue/purple colorings emerge and, if you wish for a cold snap, you might even see it exhibit a gorgeous multicolored spread. If you drop the temperature of your indoor grow room a little too much you will also see this happen; however, beautiful though it may be, this cacophony of color is a good indicator that you need to nudge the thermostat a bit. Dready Berry's preferred climate is a warm, humid one, and the plant resists mold well in these conditions. A good dose of nutrients can do well for this plant but be sure that you're not over feeding – yellowing leaf tips and wilting leaves can all be signs that you're hitting the nute bottle a little too hard. Make sure you flush with distilled water at least two weeks before harvest to make sure that your buds don't taste of chemicals. Also bear in mind that once you notice the large, dense buds begin to increase rapidly in size during the last few weeks of flowering, extra care is needed to ensure that you don't lose any of your yield to botrytis. Dready Berry will produce a substantial harvest with very resinous buds. Enjoy!

Dready Seeds, UK

Indica-Dominant

Genetics: Blueberry x White Widow

Potency: THC 16-20%

dreadyseeds.com

Though your crop may look spectacular from the vegetative stage, Dready Bob didn't choose the parentage for this strain based on looks alone. The fruity taste and aroma of their Blueberry mother and the intensity of the White Widow have both been preserved, meaning that a bowl of blue Dready Berry bud is a wholly delicious experience. Strong enough to be felt but not strong enough to leave you lying on the floor dribbling, its penchant for pain relief means that it is a good choice for medicinal users and those who enjoy a relaxing toke that tastes like dessert.

Dream Catcher

Taylor'd Genetics is an up and coming seed company based in Canada, created by breeders who have been working in the industry for two decades. They specialize in creating interesting and hardy hybrids. Their original strain Dream Catcher is named after the Native American hanging art pieces that are traditionally used to help people filter their visions while sleeping, and this strain helps to do much the same thing. The genetics are from the breeders' favorite Skunk and Afghani indicas, making it a heavy indica-influenced mix. The presence of Skunk, the original indica/sativa hybrid, brings sturdy structure and great yields to the uniformity of the Afghani indica, meaning that Dream Catcher is a grower's dream.

This plant is a bit of an all-rounder, being medium in height and density, which makes it suitable for a number of grow situations, both indoors and out. When flowering, you'll notice that the buds are wide but not too fat. As harvest time approaches they grow harder and more compact. When this happens, keep an eye on your buds for signs of mold, as the density can give rise to precisely the warm, wet conditions that mold thrives in. From the start of the vegetative stage the plants exhibit very symmetrical growth. The uniform branching makes it unnecessary to train these Dream Catcher most of the time, and the plants are exceptionally easy to clone in order to preserve the fantastic genetics. The plant is very resinous and has large trichomes that shine pleasantly and, with flowering in 67 days, Dream Catcher is a fast flowerer. Be sure not to pick the buds before they're fully ripe, as you'll be missing out on some serious quality smoke. If you're growing outdoors in the Northern hemisphere, expect harvest around October 10th.

Taylor'd Genetics,
Canada
Indica-Dominant
Potency: THC 20%
basilbush.co.uk
greenlifeseeds.com

Though the yield of this plant may not be as huge as some other hybrids, you'll walk away with a very good size stash and the quality of the nugs surpasses that of a lot of other high-yielding plants. Dream Catcher buds have a silky smoke that bursts into melon and strawberry flavors as soon as it hits your tongue. Much like its name sake, the high appeases the mind by only letting positivity and good energy into your head, but it also packs a dense body feeling that leaves you somewhere between sleep and wakefulness – a feeling that you certainly won't forget in a hurry. Check your local dispensary for some delicious nugs of Dream Catcher and you won't regret it – this strain has incredible medicinal potential, as well as a joyful and uplifting high that recreational smokers worldwide will love.

Garberville Purple Kush

Ocanabis is a Canadian grower who got hold of this classic Purple Kush strain a few years ago, and now preserves this fantastic plant. Though it originally came from the mountains of Afghanistan and Pakistan, it was bred and popularized in California, allegedly by K of Trichome Technologies. Thought to be a cross between Purple Afghani and pure Hindu Kush genetics, this strain has given rise to many variations, including Kyle Kushman's Las Vegas Purple Kush and Clone Only's GPK. It is most notably available at the Sky Blue Coffee Shop in Oakland.

There are several different phenotypes of GPK around, but a flowering time of around 55 days should be expected. This can extend to 70 days with particularly late-flowering cuts. It grows most favorably in soil or hydro set ups, but yields heavily in all media as long as it's tended to properly. As ever with Blue or Purple strains, cooler temperatures will bring out the great-looking coloration in the growing buds and make your garden look absolutely amazing.

Both smell and flavor of the resulting buds have hints of dark fruit, with underlying tones coming from the Afghani roots. The high comes on quickly with an energetic rush and a nice body high. Aches and pains melt away, which is fantastic for medicinal users as well as those just looking for some serious chill time.

Ocanabis, Canada

Indica-Dominant

Potency: THC 19%

ocanabis.com

Gordy Spice #18

Grown by Jeffman of the Blazing Pistileros Crew, Gordy Spice #18 is a variety that the celebrated Motarebel bred for an ill friend who needed a strain that would kill his pain without putting him straight to sleep. To achieve this goal, Motarebel crossed a G-13 with a Californian indica Northern Lights #5 from the BC Seed Company.

The result is a great-looking plant that's almost made for the first-time grower, as it's very resilient and forgiving. Whether your rookie error is to overfeed, under ventilate or let the tips grow too close to your bulbs, Gordy can put up with just about any-

thing. Good feeding will reward you with repeated growth spurts and super dense, frosty buds. Just before the finishing mark of 60 days, you'll get a nice purple tint on the cola and even on the leaves.

The effects of Gordy Spice #18 are said to be even stronger than Motarebel's Herijuana, so watch your intake if you're smoking this for the first time. The reason this strain was created, though, was for the ability to banish pain and relax muscles with a massive couch lock, and when you're dribbling down your own face you'll know that Motarebel succeeded.

Breeder: Motarebel Genetics

Grower: Blazing Pistileros Crew, Jeffman

Indica-Dominant

Genetics: G-13 x BCSC Northern Lights #5

irievibeseeds.com

Grape Stomper

Providing quality strains for the medical marijuana users of California, Gage Green Genetics are making a name for themselves with such strains as Blueberry Pie and this, their indica-dominant Grape Stomper. This strain has a complex and striking history, comprising the late breeder JojoRizo's Purple Elephant, a Purple Urkle Hashplant, and Chemdog Sour Diesel from Elite Seeds. The Chemdog Sour Diesel is actually a hybrid of Headband and Sour Diesel, which makes it a fantastic plant to breed from and grow.

One of the most beautiful strains in recent times, Grape Stomper has much more going for her than just her lavender trichomes. Stacked thick and dense, these swell to their fullest at 63 days. She yields well and even in a 2 gallon pot under a 1000-watt HPS indoors, she will give you an enviable stash. Great for training, as she spreads well, she could be a good choice for a SOG set up. The density and weight of her flowers might make staking necessary in the later stages so keep an eye out.

When you smoke your first home-grown Grape Stomper joint, the thick, warm, cosy effect will slide you into a relaxing stone. The pain-relieving qualities of Grape Stomper along with the gorgeous fruity taste that gives her her name will make her a favorite amongst medicinal users and everyday tokers alike.

Gage Green Genetics, USA

Indica-Dominant

Genetics: JojoRizo's Purple Elephant x Elite Seeds Chemdog Sour Diesel

Potency: THC 20%

gagegreen.org

Grubbycup's Stash

The name of this strain couldn't be more telling if it tried; bred by marijuana author Grubbycup, it's come to be a favorite of his, and therefore he always makes sure to have it as a big part of his stash. Working out of the USA, Grubbycup used a cross between a White Rhino, of Indian and Afghani indica and Brazilian sativa genetics, and a Blueberry plant for the father, and romantically introduced this to a Blackberry / Purple Lady cross. These parents not only exhibited potency and fruit flavors, but both have the thick buds and strong plant structure that Grubbycup wanted to harness.

The way the plant grows is actually its most notable feature; in later generations of seeds, a trait known as whorled phyllotaxis is common. In layman's terms, this means that there are three or four branches per node, instead of the usual two. If your seeds are of an earlier generation, this may not occur, but you definitely will see fat leaves and tight floral clusters that can be grown as a single cola or multiples, depending on how you choose to prune the plant. Due to the busy branches, and despite the strength of the plant's structure, you might find that in the flowering stages it starts to drop its arms somewhat under the weight of all those buds. If this occurs, simply stake to the branches to support them and keep an eye on them for the rest of the grow period. Netting can also be used to this effect, though it's a little more complicated. Primarily grown indoors, Grubbycup's Stash finishes in around 10 weeks and has many traits that make it suitable for a less experienced grower, including a high tolerance to bud rot and overfeeding of nutrients. However, even a toker who's been growing their own for 40 years will appreciate the unique look of these plants and the ease with which they can be brought to harvest. It's not a coincidence that these plants are the breeder's favorites, and as the buds grow to their full size in their last weeks of flowering it will probably become your plant of choice, too.

Grubbycup Stash Seeds, USA

Indica-Dominant

Genetics: (White Rhino x Blueberry) x (Blackberry x Purple Lady)

Potency: THC 17%

grubbycup.org

This strain has a very strong effect straight off, but fades somewhat and gives way to a much more long-lasting stone that creeps up on you when you think the high is almost over. The flavor is clean and tasty and the smoke is mild, and though the effects are strongly felt, it's heady enough that you can smoke this guy all day, if the fancy takes you.

Hashberry

Hashberry from Spain's celebrated Mandala Seeds was primarily created because the breeders felt that there was a lack of truly vigorous and resistant indicas on the seed market. Hashberry is a super vigorous, reliable and problem-resistant plant that is made up of Californian and North Indian (Kashmiri) genetics that were carefully selected over years of research.

Hashberry is a great indica that will grow to a medium height and is a good choice for growers with limited space, and works well in SOG set ups. This plant develops a tight and heavy head bud with dense buds located on her firm side shoots. The bud leaves have a healthy coat of THC glands, which will fill your pollinator/bubble bags very generously. Hashberry is easy to trim, heat and pest resistant, and simple to grow. Keep humidity levels and watering low during the last 2 weeks of flowering to prevent any mold from forming in the compact top buds.

Medical patients love Hashberry for its anti-anxiety, sleep-inducing capabilities, as well as a high that sets in after the first toke. The buzz starts off as lightheaded and very balanced, and then gets a little heavier near the end of the trip. Hash made from this strain is incredibly potent and can overwhelm the inexperienced toker, so be careful.

Mandala Seeds, Spain

Indica-Dominant

Genetics: Californian Hybrid x Landrace North Indian (Kashmiri)

Potency: THC 15-18%

mandalaseeds.com

Himalaya Blue Diesel

Himalaya Blue Diesel comes from the veritable hive of cannabis activity, Spain. Short Stuff Seeds is a collective of breeders committed to providing high-grade seeds at affordable prices. The company specializes in auto-flowering plants, so Himalaya Blue Diesel will flower without changing the light cycle. This is thanks to a parentage that is part Diesel Ryder, which itself is NYC Diesel crossed with the Joint Doctor's Lowryder #2, and part Blue Himalaya—an auto strain created by introducing a big Nepalese Kush to an Auto Blueberry.

Short Stuff Seeds, breeder Stitch, Spain

Indica-Dominant

Genetics: Lowyrder #2 x Blueberry x Auto Nepalese Kush x NYC Diesel

Potency: THC 18%

shortstuffseeds.com

The breeders have done well to stabilize this strain and you should see fairly consistent short plants with a hell of a lot of resin. These plants do not require a ton of space to grow to their potential and they are great indoors in small spaces such as closet grow operations. They also do well in the simplest of soil grows with organic fertilizers. They will usually only grow to around 20 to 30 inches at the very most. A plant of this size will give you around 30 grams of harvested bud. If you notice any drooping of the leaves during the early weeks of the flowering stage, a good dose of molasses can do wonders and perk your plant up greatly. Plan to harvest at around 10 weeks from seeding, as the extra couple of weeks can really make a difference and you will have the chance to enjoy the beautiful colors of this great plant. These buds, if harvested too early, can reportedly give a very racy kind of high instead of the slow, relaxing stone that they're most known and coveted for. To avoid this, and to find out why so many growers choose this strain, resist all your temptation to harvest until you're sure the buds are ready!

Like a lot of indica-dominant strains, Himalaya Blue Diesel bud has both fruity and spicy elements when smoked and packs an aromatic kick when you open your stash. The influence of the Blue family comes out slightly in the aroma as a nice hint of berries, but the biggest pleasure comes in the smoke. This is a fun bit of bud, very giggly as well as a total knockout that's likely to leave you couch locked for a good few hours. Taste it and see why it's become the favorite of so many smokers out there!

Hindu Kush

Original Seeds is a passionate breeder's collective operating out of Russia that focuses mainly on landrace genetics. For this strain, Original Seeds worked with two different Hindu Kush strains, and the Kush landrace was added to this mix to create a spectacular early-flowering homogenous phenotype. The specific genetics of these plants are unclear, though one is assumed to be from somewhere even more western and mountainous than the princely heights of Chitral in Pakistan.

This Hindu Kush strain gives small, deep green plants when grown indoors, but outdoors, the plants can reach beyond 10 feet in height. The branching forms a cone or pyramid, and will bloom into many gorgeous colors if treated with extra potassium. While purebred Hindu Kush plants are not suitable for smoking, the Kush landrace genetics in this plant provide extra resinous buds that are used by locals to make hash (charas) and well as for smoking. Hindu Kush yields dense buds and a heavy harvest, and is great for a beginner grower.

Original Seeds, Russia

Pure Indica

Genetics: Landrace
Hindu Kush

Potency: THC 17%

originalseeds.org

Hindu Kush plants have a more mild, pleasant taste than Afghani indicas and can smell of sandalwood and charas. The stone has a hypnotic, knock-out effect, though it is a quiet and contemplative high rather than one that results in petrification of the brain.

Ice Kush

Advanced Seeds are a fast-growing Spanish seed company in more ways than one; they specialize in feminized and auto-flowering strains. Ice Kush is a stellar blend of classic Kush genetics from the Hindu Kush mountains, and an equally impressive South African sativa plant. This mix produces plants with a typical indica look and shape, but with a larger production of buds and a larger size thanks to the sativa influence. The South African sativa also brings a large leaf shape and pleasing flavor to this plant.

Ice Kush can reach an indoor height of 3 to 4 feet, and an outdoor height of 6.5 to 10 feet isn't uncommon, due to the sativa influences as well as its vigorous growth patterns. This will give a yield of 350 to 450 grams per square yard. The flowering time indoors sits at around week 7 or 8 and outdoors, in the Northern hemisphere, the flowering time is late September. With a strong resistance to mildew and a distinct and pleasant aroma, this plant is great wherever you choose to grow it.

PHOTOS BY SOUTH BAY RAY

Advanced Seeds, Spain

Indica-Dominant

Genetics: Kush x South African Sativa

Potency: THC 16%

advancedseeds.com

Ice Kush smells of citrus and strawberry and has good potency as well. The buds are thick and resinous, so it is great for hash, and smokers admire its delicate mix of indica and sativa highs, meaning a pleasing body and mind buzz for tokers worldwide.

Iranian Autoflower

Iranian Autoflower (IAF) from Canadian breeder Dr. Greenthumb is an Iranian landrace that yields in a way that many auto-flowering plants do not, and by that I mean enormously. IAF produces 100 to 200 grams per plant, and is harvested in June in Canada, making this a ridiculously fast crop. Dr. Greenthumb has managed to capture the high yield characteristics of Iranian landrace plants, and has compacted them into an incredibly fast growing, auto-flowering plant that growers worldwide are recommending.

With such pace, this plant has to get its energy from somewhere, so it will need a lot of light. IAF grows to about 40 inches in height, has a flowering time of about 90 to 100 days, and the plant is ready for harvest after 6 weeks of flowering. This plant grows fine outdoors from seed, but you can also start the plant indoors and plant it outside in the spring.

IAF nugs offer a creeper-type stone. It begins with a euphoric, social high that many find quite uplifting, and then evolves into a very happy, body stone that can help you relax after a long day. If you've ever had an Iranian landrace strain before, you'll know the hashy taste that we all love for its unquestionable potency and reliability, especially for medical patients.

Dr. Greenthumb Seeds, Canada

Indica-Dominant

Genetics: Iranian Landrace Selection

drgreenthumb.com

Jet Fuel

Coming from Sativa Tim, an independent American breeder, Jet Fuel is the result of several years of work to stabilize one of his favorite crosses. With a family tree which includes Green Giant from the Brothers Grimm, Humboldt Select, and Apollo 11, another Brothers Grimm strain, it's easy to guess why this plant held such appeal for him.

Jet Fuel is an indica-dominant hybrid which nevertheless shows some sativa traits, such as leaves broken into seven distinct segments. Its plants are sturdy and short with a strong structure. Light is a big issue with these plants so be sure that they don't languish in the dark corners of your grow room. From seed to finishing should last around 2 months or less with a good amount of wattage. A healthy amount of nutrients will leave you much rewarded upon harvest, though the yield won't be particularly heavy. This is a connoisseur's strain, whose buds are worth cultivating for their density and potency alone. Growing in an organic set up could enhance the taste even further, and make your Jet Fuel harvest something really special.

Jet Fuel was so named for its gaseous smoke with undertones of orange, and a taste that's interestingly bold. The subsequent effect is a happy, giggly one that will probably leave you feeling a little scatterbrained, and is strong without being overpowering.

Sativa Tim, USA

Indica-Dominant

Genetics: Green Giant x Humboldt Select x Apollo 11

sativatimm@gmail.com

PHOTOS BY RYKA IMAGING

Kalijah

Well-respected and much renowned in their native Spain, Reggae Seeds specializes in creating strains with great taste and a potency to match. Kalijah is the offspring of DJ Short's Blue Heaven, a true Blueberry child with Thai and Afghani heritage which is no longer available in seed form. A Blue Heaven mother was bred with a male that incorporates Mexican and Afghani lines to create the indica-dominant Kalijah.

This plant can be grown indoors in relatively small containers and flourishes very well in a SOG garden. For optimum results the breeders advise leaving the plants in the vegetative stage for 5 weeks before forcing flowering. A Kalijah crop won't need a lot of nutrients and is fairly impartial about the medium it grows in, making it a good choice if you don't have much cultivation experience. Out of doors the plants branch heavily but don't grow too tall, and give beautifully-colored, compact buds. Expect harvest at the end of September in the northern hemisphere.

The much-revered Blue heritage that Kalijah enjoys comes through for the toker in the delicious smoke and the fantastic high. You'll be scrabbling around for something creative to do before sliding into a gorgeously silky high once you've exhausted yourself, but before too long you'll be reaching for the stash again!

Reggae Seeds, Spain

Indica-Dominant

Genetics: Blue Heaven x

Mexican x Afghani

Potency: THC 17%

reggaeseeds.com

Kamoto Kush

USA-based company M.G.M. Genetics is a medical cooperative passionate about creating strains that help patients. One of these is Kamoto Kush, the end result of a project left unfinished by the breeders' mentor. This Purple Kush was a mix of pure Kush and a bag seed purple male, which M.G.M. then crossed with his original i6 male over several generations until he found the phenotype that became Kamoto Kush.

With so many indica/sativa cross strains around it's easy to forget what happens when you lose the vigor of a hybrid, but Kamoto Kush, a pure indica, grows slowly in the vegetative state and needs a full 60 days in bloom to reach its potential. It is also very sensitive to temperature and, to bring it into color, you will need to expose it to lower temperatures. These plants will reward you well if grown in their favorite hydro set up.

M.G.M. Genetics, USA

Pure Indica

Genetics: Purple Kush x Indica 6

Potency: THC 19%

Though the bud isn't overly aromatic, you will detect a smell of coffee and melting hash in your nose and a sweet, oily taste in your mouth. With Kamoto Kush, couch lock is pretty much guaranteed so prepare yourself and have some good company and some tasty treats nearby, as you'll also succumb to a severe case of the munchies.

Kandahar

Ministry of Cannabis prides itself on creating exclusive strains for serious growers, and by crossing an enigmatic strain of the famous Skunk with Afghani genetics, they've achieved exactly that! The Skunk parentage was reportedly stabilized in the late 70s by Sam the Skunkman of Sacred Seeds, bringing together for the first time the taste of a sativa with the quick flowering and heavy yield of an indica; this, of course, changed the industry. The resulting hybrid brought together Afghani, Mexican and Colombian genetics to create a strain that was to become one of the most well-known in recent history. In crossing this plant with an Afghani indica, found on hillsides around the city of Kandahar which gives the strain its name, the team at Ministry of Cannabis created a strain with extremely high indica dominance (around 90%) and therefore a tendency towards dense flowering.

As would be expected from an Afghani offspring, especially when crossed with the robust Skunk, the Kandahar plant is a very consistent one to grow and is viable in a number of environments. Introducing Skunk to the equation also gives enhanced vigor. By week 8 or 9, you will have a short, bushy plant with a lot of branches, allowing you to harvest up to 500 grams from an indoor grow or 400 grams outdoors. It's interesting to note that the leaves in particular can be extremely fat compared to other plants. Both this, and the branching, means that Kandahar can grow well in a ScrOG set up if properly looked after. The vegetative stage can sit at around the 4 week period, and once you switch to a 12 on/12 off light cycle you'll notice some encouragingly steady growth. After the first 2 weeks of flowering, growth can be greatly accelerated for a week or so, but then will plateau to a steady pace to produce some fantastic buds with a lot of orange/brown hair. You can harvest anywhere from the 60 day mark.

Ministry of Cannabis, Holland

Indica-Dominant

Genetics: Afghan Kandahari x Skunk

Potency: THC 19.5 %

ministryofcannabis.com

Kandahar, when smoked, has a distinctive musky, woody smell. By the third or fourth puff you may notice an aroma of roasted walnuts. Kandahar stands apart from the majority of strains in terms of flavor alone. If your taste buds are a little more developed and you've had enough of the many fruity smokes out there, Kandahar has a great, mature taste. The high is said to be exceptionally powerful, with the ability to satisfy even the most dedicated stoner. Between the taste and the effects, Kandahar is definitely one for the serious pothead to enjoy.

King's Kush

Since 1985, Green House Seed Company has been flourishing in all kinds of respects. Now the most recognizable of all the Dutch seed companies and coffee shops thanks to their top quality genetics. King's Kush is no different, and is known for its productivity and intense, spicy aroma. A hybrid of Clone Only's fantastic and game-changing strain O.G. Kush and a Grape Ape original clone, this strain leans heavily towards the Kush traits, which is great news for anyone who gets hold of its seeds. The O.G. Kush parent, which itself is a product of ChemDawg crossed with Hindu Kush / Lemon Thai, is steeped in pot lore and hype, and has become a favorite of breeders worldwide.

When transplanting your King's Kush seedlings, ensure that the light source isn't too high from the medium as your babies will stretch to reach the light and may collapse under their own weight before you even get started. If you avoid that, this medium-sized indica will have long branches shooting both outwards and upwards, and deep green leaves tinged with purple, thanks to the Grape genetics. As with all Purple strains, the most intense colorings come out in colder temperatures, so if you're growing outside in a colder climate or choose to drop the temperature of your indoor grow room, you'll be honored with a spectacular display of violet and blues. Though these plants look fairly tame in their stature, don't be afraid to feed them like a particularly ravenous UFC fighter, as near-extreme feeding will result in enhanced flowering; you can go up to 2.3 EC in a hydro set up and 1.9 EC in a soil grow. Be sure to flush regularly to prevent excess build up in your system as this can have a negative impact on growth. The average flowering time for King's Kush is 9 weeks, and by this time, the blue-purple veins on the plant will be going wild, giving you a grow room that looks almost magical. If you're growing outside, aim to harvest at the end of October.

Green House Seed Co.,

Holland

Indica-Dominant

Genetics: OG Kush x Grape

Potency: THC 19%

greenhouseseeds.nl

King's Kush is definitely regal in its grape aroma, which is pungent, intense and tangy. It comes across as both sweet and sour, which makes for a nice change from the tons of sweet weed out there. As well as the grape smell, there are hints of lavender and moss, giving rise to a hard-hitting munchies-inducing high. When the need to feed subsides, you'll slip into a very lethargic, dreamy and mildly euphoric state that's exactly what every stoner is looking for.

Kong

Holy Smoke Seeds are flying the flag for South African breeders in Europe by offering great strains with fine genetics. One of these is Kong, which comprises the pedigrees of Magus Genetics' long-awaited Motavation, a cross of Sensi Star and Warlock, and Serious Seeds' phenomenal child of AK-47 and White Widow, known as White Russian. Motavation was chosen for its high resin production and great stature, while White Russian brought a quicker rate of flowering and huge calyxes.

Heavily indica in looks and growing, Kong has a tendency to grow immensely fat if not trimmed or trained, which can be tricky to handle. With this massive growth, however, come the huge, fluffy colas that all growers love to see and harvest, as they know that a huge return is coming their way. Though you can bring in this yield at 6 weeks, if you can hang out for 2 more weeks, it will be worth your while.

If you're wondering where the name comes from, just take a seat and have a toke, but don't expect to get up any time soon. A beast of a stone that hits you like a truck, Kong will put you out for a while whether you have one puff or twelve. If you lay your hands on a bag of Kong, keep it for a special occasion, and if you manage to get some seeds, choose your grow carefully because this plant has arms like Kong and fists to match!

Holy Smoke Seeds,

South Africa/Europe

Pure Indica

Genetics: Motavation IBL

2 x White Russian BX

Potency: 21-23%

puresativa.com

Kushdee

Holland's All Star Genetics are two breeders committed to bringing the best of the Amsterdam coffee shop strains to the wider world in the form of stabilized seeds. A big part of the Dutch cannabis community since the early 90s, these guys are using their experience to work on classic strains with a twist. Their award-winning Kushdee is a blend of the much sought-after O.G. Kush female, acquired from a friend of the breeder, and a male Spanish indica known as Alegria from the guys at Kiwi Seeds. This male was selected from the 2 best phenotypes that came from 100 Alegria seeds.

By introducing the husky Alegria to the Kush line, ASG have improved the Kush yield and its vitality, bringing an increased rate of growth as well as heftier, dank buds. One notable trait of this plant is its enormous stalks, which are necessary to hold the weight of the bigger flowers that she produces. You'll also see wider, well-shaped leaves with a lush green color. Topping this plant will increase the yield as several head colas are forced, and though it can finish in around 7 weeks if necessary, try giving your plant another 2 or 3 weeks if you have the time – it will be well worth it. Try a hand-watered soil grow for the most natural taste potency, but beware of mold and ensure that the air in your grow room is always moving.

ASG Seeds, Holland

Indica-Dominant

Genetics: Allstar Kush x Alegria

Potency: THC 18-19%

asgseeds.com

The main reason for growing Kushdee is the amazing taste and smell of the cured bud. An intricate mix of petroleum and sweet, citrus undertones in smell, the smoke is a taste sensation and the body-heavy stone is the icing on the cake.

KWT

Zenseeds is one of the premier Danish seed companies, offering a wide variety of niche strains for growers worldwide. KWT is their remake of underground breeding hero Krome's The White, which is also known as "Triangle" as it was originally a 3 way cross. Despite assumptions, KWT is not related to the infamous White Widow. The White is so named because of the astonishing crystal look it has and the frosty white buds it produces.

Easy to clone, KWT will pop roots in 5 to 7 days if you use rockwool or a bubble cloner, though she'll need a fair amount of humidity and the cubes must not be soaking wet. During the early stages of vegetative growth she does need a fair amount of attention, and responds particularly well to being topped. Though we cannot be sure of the genetics, the relatively thin branches and minor stretch point to a sativa influence. This stretch will increase during flowering so you'll need to give some attention to training, as well as staking, to give extra support to her flowering sites. Be sure to use a carbon scrubber, and though she'll look as if she's ready for harvest at the 8 week mark, 65 days is the prime time to cut.

Zenseeds, Denmark

Indica-Dominant

Genetics: Krome's The White (Triangle)

Potency: THC 19%

zenseeds.dk

Your manicured KWT buds will blow your mind. Not only are they breathtakingly beautiful, but the lemon pine scent gives way to a high that's both unique and inspiring.

L.A. Confidential

DNA Genetics, based in Amsterdam, has been producing high-quality seeds such as L.A. Confidential, a multiple-award-winning pure indica, since 2004. This plant's fantastic genes come from an Afghani landrace and an old school, killer Afghani strain from Southern California. It's often thought to be related to the O.G. Kush family, but this is a myth.

Though this plant is much imitated, there are two real L.A. Confidential phenotypes, one of which is slightly sturdier than the other. Pre-vegging is advised with this plant and doing so will maximize the amount of bud you'll get from harvest – expect around 400 grams of dried, cured bud per square yard of grow space. Both phenotypes will finish between 45 and 56 days. Don't be afraid to remove some of the fan leaves towards the end of the flowering period, as this will allow more light to reach the lower buds and stimulate their growth.

A huge part of L.A. Confidential's popularity is its ability to deliver a knock-down stone. True L.A. Confidential buds are lime green with a hint of purple and give off a piney, skunky and somewhat fleeting aroma. The extremely calm mind and body effect lasts much longer, and is complimented by a psychedelic heady trip that gives this strain such a great reputation.

DNA Genetics, Holland

Pure Indica

Genetics: California Afghani x Afghani Landrace

Potency: THC 17%

dnagenetics.com

L.A. Ultra

Founded in 2008, Resin Seeds is part of the set of young, ambitious seed companies springing up in Western Europe – in this case, Spain. The head breeder has been active in the scene since the previous decade when he ran a grow shop in Barcelona and from there, became an authority on cannabis genetics. Resin Seeds breeds, engineers and supplies product for medical marijuana users, as well as seed buyers looking for stability in their gardens. L.A. Ultra contains genetics from the well-known L.A. Confidential as well as MK Ultra, making it a very reliable all-rounder plant that has earned accolades worldwide.

Due to the heavy indica influence, plants will be fairly short and stubby, lending themselves to both indoor and outdoor environments. L.A. Confidential is resistant to mildew, and L.A. Ultra has inherited this enviable characteristic, making it a great outdoor strain. If you work indoors, don't be afraid to try this plant in an organic soil grow, as its hardiness makes it great for this sort of set up. Although a hydroponic set up isn't necessary for such a simple and easy plant, if you choose to go down that route your plant will respond well and look amazingly healthy. Flowering begins to occur between 45 and 55 days but, due to the MK Ultra parentage, the period from here to harvest isn't as short as it is for other indica strains. However, as early as 3 weeks into flowering, your plants should be covered in trichomes – patience will be necessary to wait for the right harvesting time! You'll know that you are getting there when your plants start to give off a spicy stench that stings the nostrils, but hang in there for as long as possible to ensure the most potent and dense buds you could ever wish for. An outdoor grow can be harvested in September with expected yields of 100 to 250 grams per plant, and indoors, you should take away around 350 grams of premium L. A. Ultra bud from each square yard of grow space.

Resin Seeds, Spain

Indica-Dominant

Genetics: MK Ultra x L.A. Confidential

Potency: THC 19-23%

resinseeds.net

When flowering, the buds give off a slightly spicy and fruity aroma, and often display gorgeous crystal white buds. Both L.A. Confidential and MK Ultra are known to give energetic, hard-hitting highs, and the former has been reported to give a psychedelic experience if enough is inhaled or ingested. Expect a heady and stimulating high that tokers in Spain are raving about. The 'hypnotic' stone of MK Ultra means that this is not a wake 'n bake strain – be sure to set aside some time to enjoy a decent, fulfilling trip.

Lemonberry

Fusion Seeds is a Dutch seed company producing original strains from a stock of fantastic genetics. Lemonberry is a cross between Dabney Blue, a very potent strain from the Blueberry family, and Lemon Thai Flower Time, which as the name suggests, is of Thai heritage. Crossing two strains known for their intense and distinctive flavors has resulted in a plant that's both beautiful and bursting with flavor!

Originating in the Pacific Northwest, Lemonberry is a strain for those who love DJ Short's game-changing Blueberry line. Thought to be a Thai cross acclimatized to the Hawaiian islands, Lemonberry can be grown either indoors or outdoors and can also be happily cultivated in a greenhouse set up. The indica dominance of this strain makes the plants relatively short and bushy, though the sativa of the Lemon Thai parent strain brings a medium stretch in the flowering stage that also delivers large yields of citrus-flavored buds. Due to the existence of different phenotypes, an exact flowering time is hard to estimate, but it should be in the 8 to 10 week range.

Fusion Seeds, Holland

Indica-Dominant

Genetics: Dabney Blue x Lemon Thai Flower Time

Potency: THC 19%

sanniesshop.com

The taste of this strain definitely lives up to its name, with citrus and berry tangs as well as a delightful sweetness. The high is satisfyingly balanced between body and mind with a great clarity and giggly mood.

Lowryder

You won't have to go far in the cannabis community before you run into Lowryder, the Joint Doctor's biggest gift to the growing world. The Joint Doctor created this ground-breaking plant by crossing a pure indica William's Wonder with the Seed Bank's Northern Lights #2, and as the special ingredient, a Mexican ruderalis allegedly from over 25 years ago. A feral variety of cannabis that's unable to provide a decent high on its own, ruderalis was introduced into this mix primarily for resilience and its ability to move into the flowering stage regardless of the changes of light cycles, or lack thereof.

The first strain to ever exhibit these 'auto-flowering' capabilities, Lowryder practically does away with the vegetative stage entirely, sprouting a few leaves then flowering between 17 and 20 days. This doesn't leave you with a lackluster plant, however, as Lowryder displays extremely rapid growth, with the entirety of its typical life cycle lasting only 8 weeks leaving a small but dense plant. The rest of the breeding scene scrambled to get a hold of Lowryder to breed with their strains, and since then, innumerable 'auto' versions of many seeds have become available.

On its own, though, Lowryder still produces the results: high potency and lots of resin. She has a sweet smoke and a high that can carry you right through the daytime – amazing effects from such an easy grow!

PHOTOS BY DAVID STRANGE AND GNOMES

High Bred Seeds by The Joint Doctor, Canada
Indica-Dominant
Genetics: William's Wonder x Northern Lights #2 x Mexican Ruderalis
Potency: THC 10-12%
lowryder.co.uk

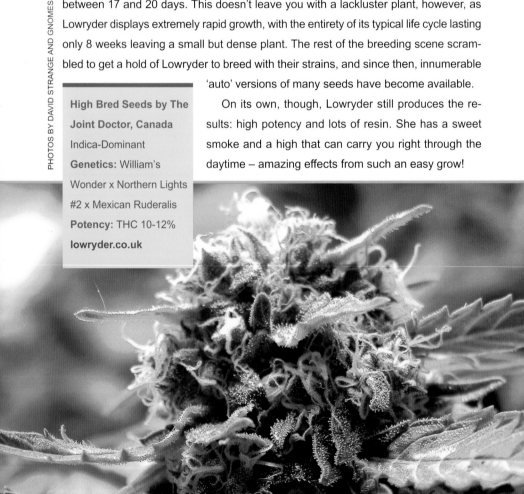

Machine Gum

Spain's Muppet Seeds is a new seed company quickly making a name for itself in the cannabis community. An offspring of Bubble Gum, which was created back in 1993, and a cross between a California indica and a California Desert Sativa, Machine Gum is mostly-indica in genetics and loves an indoor grow room. Bubble Gum in particular is known to be a highly stabilized strain with just one phenotype, which has led to its popularity as breeding stock, and it brings a uniformity and sweet taste to Machine Gum plants.

Machine Gum tends to be of medium height and though plants can grow in any environment, they will perform to their best if growers use organic cultivation methods. Chemical-free cannabis growing has become much more popular in recent years, and thanks to the growing demand for good products and decent information, there are now many great plant-based fertilizers and nutrients for both indoor and outdoor growers alike as well as books and blogs on the topic. You can also use household waste such as eggshells and coffee grounds to amend soil and encourage growth. Organic growing has also been said to give a tastier smoke and strong effects, so it can't hurt to try! Machine Gum's high resistance to pests means that you shouldn't find any little critters eating away your crop, and this makes it a good choice for a first timers. You should, however, keep your eyes peeled for any signs of mold, which can occur in warmer climates or if the humidity of your grow room is high. Keep the air inside your room moving well and make sure ventilation is one of your main priorities – especially towards the end of the flowering stage, when the sweet aroma of the plants will increase. For best results, consider pruning your plant, especially around the central cola, and it will respond well. In general, the flowering period takes place at about 8 or 9 weeks and will give a good sized harvest.

The Muppet Seeds, Spain

Indica-Dominant

Genetics: Bubble Gum x California Indica/California Desert Sativa

Potency: THC 15%

sinsemillast.com

Sniff the buds of Machine Gum and you'll be hit by the delicious sweetness that gives parent plant Bubble Gum its title. This aroma transfers into the taste of the smoked bud, and you'll also taste a smooth menthol flavor after the main hit of the smoke subsides. However, the high of this strain is even more impressive than the flavor, and renders you positively childlike: a euphoric, giggly mess with a gleeful optimism that will linger even when the stone is done.

Mad Lion OG

The AKVC Collective is an innovative cannabis collective operating in the USA that invented the world's first canned cannabis products, allowing bud to be stored in dispensaries and at patients' homes for longer periods of time. Mad Lion OG is their strain and is available in the aforementioned cans from medical dispensaries in California. Mad Lion OG has inherited the pungent aroma of its Jamaican Kush father and the delicious taste of its Skywalker OG mother.

Mad Lion OG has an incredibly pungent aroma that is almost loud in its intensity, so you'll need a good air filtration system to remain discreet. You will also appreciate the air-tight storage when carrying your cured bud and not getting busted. She grows best indoors and reaches a height of up to 6 feet. Mad Lion OG flowers in 8 weeks and takes 6 weeks to ripen after forced flowering. She prefers soil or hydroponic systems and can be viny because of her Jamaican influence, so the breeder recommends using plant netting to keep things under control. Yield can be up to 85 grams per plant depending on your lights.

AKVC Collective, USA

Indica-Dominant

Genetics: Jamaican Kush male (Kingston) x Skywalker OG clone

lakush.com

Smokers love this strain for its high that starts out very cerebral, like a pure sativa, but then, when the indica kicks in, becomes a hard couch lock experience. The smell is piney, pungent and very loud!

Mamba

Green Lantern Seeds is a fairly underground collective, run by two breeders going by the names of Manic and Inkognyto, who specialize in growing and breeding strains that will offer some respite for other patients and themselves. For this strain, Inkognyto reversed a pre-98 Bubba Kush male, to pollinate a female plant of the notorious ChemDawg strain, from noted breeder Rezdog. This resulted in a plant with 60/40 Bubba Kush to ChemDawg ratio. While the history of ChemDawg's parentage is steeped in mystique, we can assume that there's a heavy dose of indica in there, and Bubba Kush was a product of OG Kush, West Coast Dog and Old World Kush, giving us a heritage that spreads from the USA all the way to Pakistan.

Mamba, when vegetated properly, is a much denser plant than its Bubba Kush father. It also outdoes its Pops in terms of yield, but doesn't slip on the quality. The harvested nugs will be thick and tight, as well as sizeable. Be sure to give this plant plenty of light so she can produce to her full potential.

The resulting bud is stronger than is given by either of its parents, and delivers a very pleasant, heavy-headed high that will encourage sleep and keep anxiety at bay. Like Bubba Kush, the effects linger longer than your average smoke, but this is no bad thing!

Green Lantern Seeds featuring Inkognyto, Spain

Indica-Dominant

Genetics: Pre-98 Bubba Kush x ChemDawg

Potency: THC 17%

thcfarmer.com

Mamba Negra

Spain's Blimburn Seeds is an emerging seed bank focused on credibility and maximum stability of strains as well as plants with psychoactive effects. SL Green Guide and a group of noted growers have teamed up to create the company, and they have set about making a name for themselves in the increasingly-competitive Spanish seed market. The exotic and dangerously seductive-sounding Mamba Negra has come from the hands of the same people who created the celebrated Kritikal Bilbo. Mamba Negra was bred from an Afghani and Skunk offspring from Mr. Nice Seeds known as Critical Mass, an award-winning and popular breed, which was crossed with another Skunk family member for stability and great growing strength. Critical Mass is known in the growing community for both its dense, heavy-yielding plants and the punch that it carries in its smoke, and was selected as a parent strain for those very traits. The Mamba Negra now on the market is the culmination of 3 years of improvements on the original 2008 variety, and is much more stabilized thanks to that effort.

Blimburn Seeds, Spain

Indica-Dominant

Genetics: Critical Mass x Skunk

Potency: THC 18%

blimburnseeds.com

Mamba Negra seeds will give a crop of very uniform plants, as the phenotype has been so secured, and each plant will exhibit a large central baton. Flowering will bring very tight and hugely fragrant colas, the bud of which is covered in red hair and smells like ripened fruit. Though the plant is particularly well-suited to an indoor set up, it will take advantage of the extra space outside, growing large and blooming extra early. Mamba Negra is very resistant to botrytis and the size of the yield depends on your level of growing skill; proper care can result in an even larger harvest. Flowering should occur between the 55 and 65 day mark, and upwards of 500 grams of dried, cured bud can be expected from each square meter of grow space indoors. If your Mamba Negra is growing outside, it should be ready for harvest around the end of September.

This is an interesting smoke which moves through waves of physical and cerebral effects in turn, without giving you the roller-coaster effect that can sometimes occur. The taste is rich and elaborate, with hints of fruit, and the smoke is a definite lung-expander. The effects are somewhat similar to parent strain Critical Mass in that it relaxes the toker, but this is a little stronger and longer lasting. The comforting yet exciting high, coupled with the fruity and delicious smoke means that Mamba Negra is nowhere near as vicious as she sounds.

Master Kush

Amsterdam's White Label Seeds is a respected seed bank with a very loyal following. White Label provides some of the most recognizable cannabis strains on the market, as well as newer 'White' varieties of old timer strains, such as Haze and Diesel. With Master Kush, however, White Label chose not to mess with a proven winner and provided a hybrid of Indian and Afghani lines straight from separate areas of the Hindu Kush region in Northern Pakistan. Just uttering the name 'Kush' will have most stoners frothing at the mouth, and this strain is no different. Tokers worldwide enjoy the smooth flavor of this beauty.

Master Kush plants tend to favor indoor set ups, and once your friends find out you are growing a Kush plant it might become necessary to have a year-round grow op going just to keep up with demand. The plant is happy enough in a simple soil set up, and though it can suffer if you get carried away with the nutrients, it is a very straightforward plant to grow. Master Kush is mold resistant, but as always you should keep your grow room well-ventilated. As with all indicas, your plants won't grow overly tall, but will grow strong and fairly bushy. Expect the high resin production for which all Kush plants are known, and the reliably great yields. As these plants are so sought-after and hardy, you might want to consider growing them in a hydroponics set up, in which they've been said to do notably well. Their vigorous growth can be complimented by a regular feeding and nutrient regime and this could help you to get the very best out of what is already a great plant. Also, regardless of how the bud actually turns out, telling people that you have hydro Master Kush will suddenly make you a very popular friend, and the street value will go through the roof.

White Label Seeds, Holland

Indica-Dominant

Genetics: Hindu Kush x Hindu Kush

Potency: THC 16%

whitelabelseeds.com

Serious smokers will recognize the distinctive flavor of hand-rubbed charas hashish, which is actually made from Hindu Kush weed in Northern Pakistan and Central Afghanistan. The high of this strain avoids the mind-numbing effects of a lot of indica-heavy strains and won't leave you totally baked and unable to spell your own name. It does, however, pack a fairly serious body stone with a euphoric, giggly result. Expect an incredibly smooth smoke, especially through a pipe, with a little bit more of a cough lingering if enjoyed through a bong. From a medical perspective, Master Kush can help those struggling to get a good night's sleep or suffering from stress.

Matanuska Tundra

As the celebrated producers of the popular Yumbolt strain, Sagarmatha Seeds are highly thought of amongst growers and breeders alike. Based in Holland, they've been established since 1994 and consistently impress the industry with their innovative breeds and the purity of their genetics. Matanuska Tundra, also known to some people as Alaskan Thunder Fuck, is an indica-heavy plant from the Matanuska Valley of the Alaskan Northlands. Thanks to the quality of this strain, the seeds are highly sought after and can be more expensive than other seeds.

Matanuska Tundra can be grown in any sort of grow set up, coming as it does from the harsh surroundings of Alaska. Average flowering time is around 60 to 70 days. It's relatively small and will only grow to between 20 and 30 inches, making it great for an indoor grow or one that has to be fairly covert. If growing indoors, be sure to watch the internodes with a close eye – once there are between 4 and 7 inches in length, it's time to force flowering.

Sagarmatha Seeds, Holland

Indica-Dominant

Potency: THC 18%

highestseeds.com

The rock-hard buds are gorgeously smooth and chocolaty in their smoke and the high is seductively sedative. This smoke will leave you feeling like a chubby teenager overdosing on hot chocolate and melting into a big comfy couch: absolutely fantastic.

Mazar-I-Sharif

Bomba Seeds are an independent seed company based in the Ukraine. Their Mazar-i-Sharif plant is a pure, landrace indica that was discovered by a soldier who fought during the Soviet War in Afghanistan. This nameless soldier had strong anti-war sentiments, but had to fight regardless, and found solace in one interest he shared with some of the Afghan civilians he met – a love of good hashish. Before returning to the former USSR he made sure to collect seeds from his favorite plants in the region and brought them home. These seeds were passed on to Bomba Seeds who now offer them to the public.

If grown outdoors, as nature intended, these plants become indica giants that reach heights of 10 to 13 feet with a classic wide leaf shape. A yield of 50 to 70 ounces per plant isn't uncommon, and harvest time is early December to early January. The buds are heavy and the yield is large, so be prepared to stake your garden. Mazar likes the cold weather and is hardy, so growers can plant them outside and harvest them in December despite the cold weather. These plants have been known to grow in the snow and can survive even very brutal winter weather.

Bomba Seeds, Ukraine

Pure Indica

Genetics: Landrace Mazar-i-Sharif

Potency: THC 17%

bombaseeds.com

Mazar-i-Sharif has a pungent, intense aroma with some classic Afghan sweetness thrown in for good measure. The high is mellow, but over-indulgence can produce a mind-warping couch lock effect, so be careful.

Mendo Purp

PureBred Growers is a U.S.-based collective of breeding experts, and for this strain, the team has further developed a plant originally bred five years ago by the Rebel Lion Collective in California. A triple cross of Purple Urkle, Grape Ape and Granddaddy Purps, all members of the Blue family, Mendo Purp has been a favorite of growers and tokers alike since its release and has now been made into a Cali classic by PureBred Growers.

This plant isn't fussy and enjoys being cultivated in both hydroponic and soil-based set ups. Your choice of medium dictates what exact colorings it produces; soilless grows giving a dark purple tinge and soil grows giving royal gold and purple hues with hardly any green. These gorgeous plants will grow between 2 and 3 feet and should finish fully in 9 to 10 weeks, and, unusually, don't produce a higher yield if grown outdoors rather than indoors. Don't use a bucket any larger than 5 gallons, as the root mass stays fairly small. The smell will be extremely strong in the last weeks of flowering, so be aware!

PureBred Growers, USA

Indica-Dominant

Genetics: Purple Urkle x Grape Ape x Granddaddy Purps

purebredgrowers.com

A secret breeder's tip is to take a nice fat J of Mendo Purp to the top of a hill and finish the whole thing before you snowboard down. You'll find yourself boarding on the fluffiest snow imaginable, and it doesn't even hurt that much when you stack it – awesome!

Montreal Chemo

Trichome Pharm, based in Canada, comprises a group of licensed medical marijuana growers and breeders keen to make access to both quality product and accurate information easier for those who need it. They are currently in the process of creating a research program with a view towards launching a database that plots different strains against the symptoms that they can help relieve. In the meantime, they have produced Montreal Chemo, which as the name suggests, is an original Canadian strain with very strong effects designed for medicinal users. Part of the celebrated Chemo family, Montreal Chemo has been popular in the Quebec cannabis community for almost 15 years. The strain is particularly noted for its pain management properties and strong appetite stimulation, and is one of the strains of choice for compassion societies.

The genetic indica dominance is easy to see as soon as the plant enters the vegetative stage and begins to exhibit heavy stalks, hollow stems and the particular strength in structure that is not seen in sativa-dominant hybrids. Though the robustness of the plant means that it is able to grow in almost any scenario, it does produce especially well when grown with the SOG technique. If this is not your own choice of technique, Montreal Chemo will also produce well when allowed to grow into a slightly larger plant, and as such, enjoys lots of room and a slightly heavier feeding regime. These crops do tend to need a little more love than other indicas, and if not taken care of properly can be susceptible to pests and diseases.

Trichome Pharm, Canada

Indica-Dominant

Potency: THC 23%

trichomepharm.com

These plants respond very well to LST (low stress training), which tricks the plant into forming new growth along the flower stems to push new shoots out to reach the light. This basically involves pulling some of the more dominant shoots downwards, to make the plant forget that some of its tips are close to the light. To remedy this, it pushes other growth out towards the light, or creates new light-seeking stems. The mechanics of this technique are similar to that of topping, though the process is very different.

Near harvest time, your Montreal Chemo buds will be coated with thick and oily resin, making it a great crop to produce hash from. Your grow room will be full of pine forest aromas just before harvest, and though your growing method of choice will affect the taste, you should notice earthy and fruity tones within the smoke. The resulting high is both heavy and narcotic, while remaining mellow. A great one for connoisseurs and medical patients.

Mr. Nice (G-13 x Hash Plant)

Named after Howard Marks, a British hashish importer and one of the most prolific contemporary cannabis activists, this strain from Holland's masters of breeding, Sensi Seeds, comprises some pretty serious genetics. While the male parent, Hash Plant, is a direct descendant of one of the best genotypes to come out of the Hindu Kush region, the female parent, G-13, is almost mythical, such is the legend surrounding its origins. It's the story that every stoner will tell their kids, the one where the U.S. government breeds an ultra-potent strain only to have a cutting liberated by a weed-

Sensi Seeds, Holland

Indica-Dominant

Genetics: G-13 x Hash Plant

Potency: THC 20%

sensiseeds.com

loving lab technician, which then becomes the hottest property amongst the counter-culture stoners. We'll never know the truth, but either way, the quality of G-13 has become famous in its own right, and its original pairing with Hash Plant was available in limited edition seeds in the 90s and was brought back to much celebration by Sensi in 1999.

These days, Mr. Nice seeds give rise to solid crops which won't grow any taller than about 50 inches but can yield up to 100 grams of premium indica bud per plant. Expect flowering in about 60 days and be sure not to overdose them in the earlier stages of growth – just let them do their own thing! Also try not to over water the plant as it's simply unnecessary and can only damage your grow. These plants love a lot of light, and the more you give them, the more they will produce for you, but be careful that the leaf tips don't get too close to the bulb or they'll burn. With such dense buds, it's imperative to ensure that ventilation in your grow room is sufficient, and humidity is kept at 40% or below during the second half of flowering, as stagnant, wet air can give rise to mold inside the colas. Invest in more fans to ensure a good flow of air if you think this is a concern in your set up, and keep an eye on the humidity at all times.

Mr. Nice is a smoke for the heaviest of tokers, those who could take a whole cross-joint of Skunk without even batting an eyelid. The 'double Afghani' taste gives you the ultimate body stone and knocks you off your feet. Depending on your tolerance you might enjoy a few hours of lazy euphoria and a bit of couch lock, or you could lose all motor function and be totally macraméd to your chair. Either way, it's not the best choice for a rookie smoker, but the experienced will love it.

Mt. Cook

It doesn't take a genius, or for that matter, a DEA detective, to figure out where Kiwi Seeds are based, even if they do operate from Holland. For this strain they've gone back to their roots, naming this mainly-indica hybrid after the highest mountain in New Zealand, Mount Cook – or Aoraki as the Maoris would call it. It's not exclusively a Kiwi strain because it has an Afghani/Thai mother and a father that's half Northern Lights and half Hash Plant, but as that gene pool sounds so promising, we won't hold it against them!

As is typical for such an indica-influenced hybrid, Mt. Cook plants grow beautiful dark green leaves on sturdy, thick branches, and give heavy buds when flowering rolls around at about the 50 day mark. However, these flowers are often so heavy that you will need to lend some extra support to the top branches and the cola. A stake will work just fine, or some growers like to use supportive netting to make their Mt. Cook plants really secure. Though there are a couple of phenotypes, the only real difference is that one exhibits slightly more Thai traits and one shows slightly stronger Northern Lights traits; both grow well in the same situations. Mt. Cook is well suited to indoor grow rooms, and if you favor the SOG technique this makes a good choice, though it does take a little longer than some indicas to finish. Flowering should occur in 58 days or less. It also takes fantastically to a hydroponic or aeroponic set up, so if your budget is large enough to accommodate the higher start up costs of a hydroponic grow, you could try an ebb and flow system with grow rocks as a medium. Mt. Cook plants can withstand relatively large doses of nutrients without succumbing to nutrient burn, but as ever, be careful that you don't get too carried away or all your hard work will be ruined. In hydroponic set ups especially, the need to ensure proper environmental temperatures and nutrient levels is high. Your yield should be enhanced by a more technical set up, but even in a soil grow, yield should be along the lines of 450 grams per square yard.

Kiwi Seeds, Holland

Indica-Dominant

Genetics: Afghani/Thai x Northern Lights/Hash Plant

Potency: THC 18%

kiwiseeds.com

When smoked, these buds have a very earthy taste, crammed with rich flavor. It's somewhat reminiscent of real Hash with a little more depth. The stone is just as serious as the taste, with the high hitting heavily and immediately before mellowing out to a beautiful body stone with a heavy feeling appreciated most by those who enjoy a few hours of couch lock!

Northern Light Special

Holland's Spliff Seeds produces quality seeds and prides itself on offering fantastic customer service. With Northern Light Special, they have a new take on the legendary Northern Lights family. First bred in Seattle from a Californian plant, Northern Lights is a favorite amongst breeders due to its big, potent buds and fantastic resin production. This ancestor is a very heavy indica hybrid, and comes from a mix of Afghani, the famed 'true' indica, Hindu Kush, and Thai. Breeders should be aware that there are two phenotypes: one short and stalky with a compact bud structure and large fan leaves, and another that is reminiscent of a lemon skunk plant.

As expected from a strain with such dominant indica genetics, Northern Light Special plants are short in stature and compact enough to make them great indoors. They are easy to control in a small grow room, but also produce a great yield for plants of their size, making them a good choice for those concerned with getting a big harvest from the smallest amount of grow space. They also grow well outside, where they won't grow as leggy or tall as some other plants, and they aren't too fussy about which type of fertilizers you use on them. They can sometimes have a bit of a stretch, but nothing that becomes too invasive on the rest of your space. In fact, a Northern Light Special crop is said to be mostly headache-free in almost any environment. This makes them a particularly good choice for a newbie grower who may not know what to do if their plant is plagued with botrytis or does not respond to nutrient feedings. Also, thanks to the parentage of Hindu Kush, which produces dense, compact buds covering the branches from stalk to tip, Northern Light Special is a huge resin producer and grows very quickly – a beautiful sight for the eyes of any grower!

Spliff Seeds, Holland

Indica-Dominant

Genetics: Afghani x Hindu Kush x Thai

Potency: THC 18%

spliffseeds.nl

This plant has a Skunk-like smell, with an earthy honey musk odor, but tastes very sweet. The high is a buzzy, full-body stoned feeling that has smokers in Holland hooked. Due to this soothing high, medicinal marijuana users smoke Northern Light Special to relax and combat chronic pain. The warm buzz is like a giant hug with a tendency towards contemplative aftershocks. It can also result in a serious case of couch lock if you're not too careful, so make sure the remote is within arm's reach before you spark up. You can also use the buds to make hash oil to create canna-cookies or space brownies, both of which are fantastically potent – so be careful that you don't get carried away and scarf the whole batch or you may never get up again.

Northern Skunk

Peak Seeds of Canada is based in British Columbia and aims to bring integrity and a personal touch to the seed business, with an inspiring breeding motto of "Preserve the original, perfect the progeny." Their Northern Skunk is the result of breeding the much-loved Northern Lights #5 from the BC Seed Company with Peak's own Skunk male plant, to give a very potent strain that's also easy to grow.

The individual parent plants of Northern Skunk were chosen for their lateral branching, stocky stature and low odor during the vegetative stage. All of these desirable traits were preserved in the offspring. A short plant which has flowers at about 8 weeks indoors, Northern Skunk loves organic soil grows that are fortified with organic fertilizers and responds particularly well to molasses in the flowering stage. It can be finished in 9 weeks but if you can wait until day 77 (you'll be happy you did).

Peak Seeds, Canada

Indica-Dominant

Genetics: Northern Lights x Pure Skunk F1

Potency: THC 20%

peakseedsbc.com

The sweet skunkiness emitted from these buds when crushed is a harbinger of their effect; a very Skunk-like body relaxant that is adaptable to many situations because the energy of the high saves you from being locked to the couch and lasts for two hours or more.

Obsession

Spanish company World of Seeds is comprised of a multicultural group of horticultural and biology enthusiasts with an interest in cannabis. As well as operating a seed bank, the team works on original strains, one of which is Obsession, the name of which gives you a clue about how much this crew cares about producing high quality strains. After many years of crossbreeding, the World of Seeds experts were finally satisfied enough to release this one to the market. They took a plant which held the genetics of three amazing strains – White Rhino, Black Domina and Jack Herer – and crossed it with a Pakistani indica known as Gilgit Valley. Thanks to this mélange of pedigrees, Obsession quickly became a sensation among cannabis connoisseurs.

Highly resistant to all pests and with a majority indica influence, Obsession is an ultra-stable strain. It is best suited to growing indoors, where it finishes fully in 9 weeks, but can also be grown outdoors when it should be ready at either the end of September or the first week of October. The success of your outdoor grow will depend on your location, as Obsession doesn't particularly enjoy colder climates.l If you're in an area that experiences extremes of weather and temperature, you might choose to house your Obsession plants in an indoor garden. If so, ensure that each plant has a good position with access to a lot of light, even on the lower branches, and you'll see some good growth and substantial flowering. If your budget doesn't extend to purchasing a massive amount of bulbs or LEDs, store-bought or homemade reflectors can be put to good use in this kind of situation, as they bounce the light into parts of the set up that might otherwise be relatively dark. Obsession crops are usually great yielders as they are very resilient, and work very well in mild climates. Be sure not to harvest your crop too early and you should find yourself with a respectable stash of some delightful buds with a great aroma.

World of Seeds, Spain

Indica-Dominant

Genetics: Gilgit Valley x (White Rhino x Black Domina x Jack Herer)

Potency: THC 15-20%

worldofseeds.com

Flavorsome and very fragrant, Obsession buds might leave you totally devoted to them like an emotional lover thanks to their mouthwatering smell and wholesome taste. Once the pleasure of the taste subsides, the chilled-out high will take a gentle hold of you and cradle you into submission. A good choice for social smoking, the buzz won't leave you incapacitated or overly introspective. This strain is well-suited to medicinal users thanks to its mellow but relaxing high which is a great elevator of mood and so combats depression.

Olivia Kush

OtherSide Farms is a medical marijuana information center in the USA that dispenses education about cannabis as well as how to grow. The team is extremely passionate about providing professional and high quality products, and this commitment shines through in this original strain. Olivia Kush is an indica-dominant mix of the Hindu Kush and Skunk lines, the latter of which is known for its vigorous growth and potent high.

These short plants are very hardy and begin to look extremely bushy towards the end of the vegetative stage. Olivia Kush is more than happy in an organic soil-based

OtherSide Farms, USA

Indica-Dominant

Genetics: Hindu Kush x Skunk

Potency: THC 20%

othersidefarms.com

grow, and given good quality soil and the right amount of feeding, can be a fantastic yielder. She isn't fussy and is a fast finisher. She should be done completely in around 8 weeks, when her deep green colas exhibit hints of purple here and there.

Olivia Kush has a very thick smoke and is a definite cougher, so don't feel like a rookie toker when you're reaching for that glass of water. The effects, though, will make you feel like a newbie: a total knock out stone that hits like a brick wall, making it ideal for the medicinal users this strain was designed for.

P-91

Stoney Girl Gardens is the philanthropic mission of a socially conscious group of card-holding legal growers of medical marijuana who have been operating in Oregon since 1999. Stoney Girl Gardens is passionate about creating true breeding strains and providing 100% organic seeds, with a master breeder who's been in the game for over 40 years. The company even provides free growing classes, such is their dedication to the cause, and their P-91 strain is a classic for those who need a heavy-duty medicinal plant. The genetics are somewhat mysterious, as the original seeds were obtained from a university professor who had first bred them. As the 'new G-13,' this supposedly came from a government-sponsored breeding program at a University in Southern California that is so top secret that, for all intents and purposes, it doesn't exist. The story goes that the professor handed the seeds over to Stoney Girl in exchange for some of its Berkeley Blues seeds, and that this strain became a great addition to their breeding program, giving rise to their Pit Bull and Hog's Breath families, among others.

Stoney Girl Gardens,

USA

Indica-Dominant

Potency: THC 28%

gro4me.com

Happily grown either indoors or outdoors, P-91 has a lot of energy and bursts into life very quickly. She's easy to grow right through to harvest, and will grow to between 4 and 6 feet tall. Her favorite temperatures are those of Cali and if you can keep her in conditions between 70 and 80 degrees Fahrenheit she'll be seriously stoked. If you obtain these seeds to start your own medicinal garden, you'll be pleased to hear that she's an easy one to clone, with the clones taking quickly and easily once planted. Flowering lasts around 40 days and just before you chop your plants you'll see huge, deep green leaves with bud that's accordingly massive. The flowers are very tight and heavy and, if you grow outside, you'll see a lot of pure pink hairs on the already-beautiful nugs.

It should serve as a warning to all potential recreational smokers of P-91 that this strain is massively potent. As with most pain-killing strains, this will put you out completely and therefore is not for use any time other than before bed. The intention of breeding P-91 was to offer a much-needed respite for those suffering most: HIV/AIDS patients, cancer patients, extreme addicts, sufferers of severe pain and terminal patients. As such, the stone hits very rapidly and lasts for a long time. The smoke tastes musky and dense, with hints of grapefruit and spice, and gives an almost immediate couch lock effect. This is effective enough to be recognized by doctors as a morphine replacement treatment, so be very wary before you toke.

Peace Maker

If you're actively involved in the cannabis community you'll be familiar with *Treating Yourself* magazine, a publication launched to promote the responsible use of medical marijuana. Finest Medicinal Seeds, the publishers of this fine mag, also run a seed bank from their base in Canada, and one of their strains is the famous Peace Maker from the 90s. Bred in Holland, this combination of Super Skunk and White Widow is a hybrid with Indian and Brazilian heritage, as well as a genetic link to the formidable Skunk #1.

The name Peace Maker has become synonymous with big yields, short flowering times and great taste. The plant has a short and steady internode with a bushy buildup and short, strong branches. One of the most distinctive traits of this strain is the sharp, serrated profile of its leaves that may remind you of sharks' teeth. It's best to grow Peace Maker in a hydroponic system, specifically an open system using rockwool flakes with no recycling of water, to achieve its maximum yield and potency. If you're more interested in cultivating the best possible taste, give soil a go, and even think about using organic fertilizers and nutrients. The vegetative stage should last around 36 to 40 days, and consider that, while 8 weeks is the general harvest point, leaving the crop for an extra week will increase the potency and sweetness of the extra-heavy buds. Despite the weight of these, staking shouldn't be necessary thanks to the strength of the plant itself. Resin will start to form in the third week of flowering and peak at 8 weeks. This will make for an extra sticky harvest, so be sure to wear gloves and cover your eyes when you're chopping. Failing to do so can result in a horribly powerful contact high and, should you wipe your eyes with resin-covered hands, you find yourself not only with a stinging face but also suffering from the worst kind of red eye.

Finest Medicinal Seeds, Canada

Indica-Dominant

Genetics: Super Skunk x White Widow

Potency: THC 17%

finestmedicinalseeds.com

The taste of Peace Maker is reminiscent of summer fruits with a candy aftertaste. When ripened for that little extra time, a hint of spice is added to this mix making for a spectacularly layered flavor. These older buds will give a very heavy stoned feeling that lasts a long time and gives great respite from MS and arthritis. Even the younger nugs deliver a decent punch and a full-body muted buzz that will make it near-impossible to tap dance around the room but should leave you in the right mood for good company and a funny movie.

Pennsylvania Purple

Pennsylvania Purple is an underground strain circulating on the East Coast that is producing quite a lot of buzz both locally and internationally through word of mouth and online forums. Pennsylvania Purple is currently only available in the USA, but the breeders, who prefer to remain anonymous due to the draconian laws of their home states, are planning to tissue culture this cultivar in the hopes of making it more commercially available. For now, just remember that if you get the chance to buy a clone of this beauty or to take a puff on some of her buds, take it. She's a great plant.

Unknown East Coast Grower, USA

Indica-Dominant

Potency: THC 17%

Produced by a collective of East Coast growers, Pennsylvania Purple is a 30% sativa and 70% indica strain that grows well indoors and outdoors. Outdoor growers can expect a dark purple coloration to appear naturally as temperatures drop and the plant matures. To get purple colors indoors, use Purple Maxx (foliar) nutrients, although a drop in grow room temperature can also induce darker purple colors. Pennsylvania Purple likes the cold temperatures of her home state, grows to about 4 feet tall, and works well in SOG set ups. She can also do very well in hydro grow rooms and in soil gardens, though amending the soil before you plant the seedlings can give her a great springboard to start from. As tempting as it is to shower these darlings with the best nutrients on the market, don't go mad or you'll ruin her natural beauty with nute burn. Expect a flowering time of 60 days and a time of 72 to 75 days for her to ripen after forced flowering with a moderate yield. Quality not quantity is the name of the game when growing Pennsylvania Purple and although the yield is low, even a handful of cured, dried nugs will have the most hardened toker weeping with joy. Bud this beautiful is always in high demand so if you get a hold of any seeds, you can land yourself a very lucrative crop.

Pennsylvania Purple has a smooth, fruity and sweet taste that has delicious tones of grape, as is common with purple plants. The high is clear, physically relaxing, and evenly matched between the mind and body, allowing users to chill out and be creative while they are stoned. Artists especially will appreciate this kind of high. The breeder recommends flushing the plant during the last 10 days of flowering with half a teaspoon of molasses per gallon of water to encourage a healthy, great tasting harvest.

Pinkbud

Secret Garden Seeds has broken new ground with Pinkbud: an auto-flowering SOG-specific strain, something not seen regularly in the expansive cannabis market. This strain was the company's first attempt at making a colorful variety that met these criteria, and to do so, they used a three-way hybrid of LowAsis, M. JEMS and Diesel Ryder. This crossing increased the flavor of LowAsis and preserved the beautiful coloring traits that JEMS are known for.

Pinkbud plants have it all: large colorful buds from JEMS, heavy resin production from Diesel Ryder, and the great flavor of LowAsis. Plants are very uniform, which is a must for any auto-flowering SOG system. The plants average at about 20 inches in height, have a distinct main cola dominance and limited branching. Planting at 4 plants per square foot yields an impressive canopy of large buds, with beautiful pink, purple, red, and green colors. Despite being formulated for a SOG set up, the plants also do well outdoors thanks to their resistance to mold and frost.

The smoke of Pinkbud is light and pleasant, and the high is a mellow one but don't expect to get much done if you smoke in the morning!

Secret Garden Seeds, UK

Indica-Dominant

Genetics: LowAsis x M. JEMS x Diesel Ryder

secretgardenseeds.com

Puna Blue

Supreme Beans is a Hawaii-based breeder dedicated to finding the best plants of the beautiful Pacific islands, stabilizing their genetics and then bringing them to the wider cannabis community. Puna Blue is a strain that was given to him by a grower from Hawaii's Big Island with unknown genetics, but the name may hint at some relation to another Hawaiian strain, Puna Budder from TH Seeds, as well as some heritage that may include DJ Short's famous Blueberry. We can be sure, however, that PB is a 75/25 indica-sativa hybrid with all the quality typical of the plants from the islands.

This plant tends to grow with one huge main cola rather than several smaller ones, and as is the case with most Blue plants, has a hefty density. It also grows quite quickly with especially fast flowering, which can be expected at around 8 weeks. Although the gorgeous coloring will start to come through at the end of flowering, lower temperatures can bring the indigos out even further and leave you with some seriously good-looking bud. Humidity can be an issue with such dense buds, so make sure that there isn't too much moisture in your grow room.

This must be what they smoke in Hawaii, as the tangy nugs give rise to a heavy, narcotic but social stone that makes the concept of 'island time' seem totally normal.

PHOTOS BY SOUTH BAY RAY

Supreme Beans, USA

Indica-Dominant

Genetics: Hawaiian x Afghani

Potency: THC 17%

supremebeans.net

Purple Pineberry

Canada's Secret Valley Seeds knows what is important to commercial growers, and produces strains bred from only the best of their seed stash, that deliver these sought-after traits. While their Hardcore and Top Dollar plants are quick-flowering and high-yielding to allow for very productive grow rooms, Purple Pineberry is a little more deep in its purpose. Though its history is either cloaked in secrecy or genuinely unknown to the breeders, we can be sure that it is an indica-dominant hybrid with some definite resilience in growing.

Purple Pineberry is a hardy plant that flowers quickly and braves humid Canadian summers well thanks to its resistance to mold. When flowering comes around, it will produce chunky, solid buds that exude a great aroma of pine. These can be harvested after 6 weeks indoors, or around September 20th in an outdoor garden.

Purple Pineberry buds have a very distinctive smell and can give rise to a harsh but lightly sweet smoke. It has a very pleasant mellow high which is energizing and won't pull your energy levels down. Secret Valley Seeds are constantly working on newer versions of this strain as well as more innovative ways to cross breed with it to ensure its great genetics are retained for future generations of Pineberry.

Secret Valley Seeds, Canada

Indica-Dominant

Potency: THC 18%

greenlifeseeds.com

Red Flame Kush

Red Flame Kush is SinsemillaWorks' latest indica strain. The team of breeders has crossed a Purple Kush female with a Blue Moonshine male to make a killer hybrid and are currently pollinating and testing it with a strong indica plant. They will have a stabilized strain soon, so keep an eager eye out for it. Initial results show a strong plant with a blend of both parent strains, and it flowers rapidly in just seven weeks. She has great colors coming from both the Purple Kush and Blue Moonshine parents, and a classic indica resiliency from the Blue Moonshine, which loves outdoor and organic systems. Expect to see this strain in the medical clubs, and check out SinsemillaWorks' videos for help and advice on growing their strains.

Growers should expect typical indica growth patterns with good-sized fan leaves and a stocky structure. The plant is short and stout with tight, rock hard resinous buds. Red Flame Kush is resilient and grows outdoors in cold weather or indoors in all sorts of systems. The taste is incredible if the plant is organically grown.

PHOTOS BY GIORGIO ALVAREZZO

SinsemillaWorks!, USA

Indica-Dominant

Genetics: Purple Kush x Blue Moonshine

Potency: THC 17%

sinsemillaworks.com

The taste and flavor are potent owing to the strong indica background. Blue Moonshine is related to the White Widow family and inherits its potent high, along with its dense trichomes. The high is narcotic and hits the body like Mike Tyson.

Redd Cross

Genetics Gone Madd is a medical cooperative operating out of the US, working on new strains to offer the highs that their customers need. The late Dan Christensen, a passionate GGM breeder who unfortunately passed away recently, did much of the development of Redd Cross, which comprises genes of an unknown Afghani indica and the almost equally enigmatic Spirit of 76, apparently one of the first strains grown on the hills of California.

Named via one of GGM's strain-naming competitions, Redd Cross seeds grow into very compact plants that should not be topped, as this could result in overcrowding of the colas. Laborious efforts to breed structural integrity into the plants has resulted in a sturdy, solid trunk and branches, which should eliminate the need for any sort of containment to shoulder the weight of her heavy top. Also be sure not to over water your crop, as Redd Cross is drought and cold tolerant but can get flooded easily.

Expect to harvest after 60 days indoor, or the first week of September if exposed to the sun, and after a few weeks of curing kick back to enjoy the immediate heat rush of a high that will hit your body. The sweet smoke will elevate your blood pressure for a short time but also gives great relief from bone and nerve pain.

Genetics Gone Madd, USA

Indica-Dominant

Genetics: Spirit of 76 x unknown Afghani Indica

Potency: THC 19%

facebook.com/Genetics-GoneMad

Sannie's Herijuana IBL

Holland's Sannie's Seeds are dedicated to producing quality strains for the cannabis connoisseur, and have definitely hit the nail on the head with this strain. Sannie's Herijuana IBL, originated from Canada's Woodhorse Seeds and was perfected by noted breeder Motarebel. This plant was created from a 2006 batch of seeds through years of selecting the best phenotypes, backcrossing them and then breeding them with the company's original mother plant. This has given rise to a highly stabile and sought-after plant, much like Motarebel's other noted strains Star Kush and White Molokai.

Sannie's Seeds, Holland

Indica-Dominant

Genetics: Killer New Haven Strain x Petrolia Headstash

Potency: THC 20-25%

sanniesshop.com

Herijuana is an extremely popular strain throughout the cannabis community because of its fast growing pattern and desirable branching. Despite exhibiting a development more typical of a sativa-dominant plant, this strain blooms like an indica with vigorous branching that makes it very suitable for a ScrOG set up. Your Herijuana IBL plants should be ready to move into the flowering stage around the 8 week mark, and a minimum vegetative cycle of 6 weeks is recommended for optimum yield. The plant continues to grow for a couple of weeks into the flowering cycle and begins to form golf-ball shaped buds that are as beautiful as they are dense. These will be rock hard by the last few weeks of flowering and, thanks to the wide internodal spacing, produce tons of resin. As ever, be sure to exercise caution when harvest comes around, as dealing with such resinous plants can bring on a ridiculously strong contact high; gloves and goggles are always recommended. The plants shouldn't grow beyond 4.5 feet in height but will yield between 400 and 500 grams per square yard of grow room.

The taste of this strain is delightful, as it contains hints of both dark coffee and wood, and the stone is just as good: an intense, narcotic couch lock high that pulls down on the eyelids. Smokers who are new to the scene should exercise caution, as this is an extremely potent strain, and can take even a daily toker by surprise. It's known as a one-hit-wonder, and not because it had a popular song and some fleeting fame in the 80s; just a few puffs of this can lay you right out. Just take it easy and enjoy the feeling. Remember, you don't have to smoke it all at once!

SDOGnesia

Ultimate Seeds is a fairly young seed bank offering the top strains, including great originals. For this exclusive strain, Ultimate has raised the bar for great genetics. The previously popular Sour Diesel x OG Kush cross was brought back to life, and brought with it an expansive family tree that includes 1991 Chemdawg, Northern Lights, Super Skunk, Hawaiian, Diesel, OG Kush and Lemon Thai. That makes one mean family gathering even before you consider that this plant was then married to Ultimate Seeds' favorite Amnesia Haze cut. The award-winning and exotic Amnesia Haze is of Laotian, Hawaiian and Jamaican heritage, and is known to give an intense, lingering body buzz that has made it the choice of many heavy smokers. Given this rich gene pool, it's easy to see why SDOGnesia is regarded as such a high-quality strain.

As is often the case with a young strain that hasn't yet been fully stabilized, there are many phenotypes of SDOGnesia, exhibiting a variety of traits. However, all of these phenotypes produce plants that are extremely shiny, as if always wet. This is due to the huge trichome production and should be cause for celebration rather than concern! This also means that the plant is extremely sticky, so caution should be used when harvesting or trimming, as a massive and unpleasant contact high can result from over-handling. SDOGnesia is a relatively quick finisher, and flowers in 8 to 10 weeks depending on how and where you choose to grow your crop. Just before harvest you'll be treated to a lingering, sweet aroma from your grow room. Once chopped, these buds will mature with an even more delicious smell. Your yield should be a heavy one, especially if the plant is grown outside where it has more room to spread its roots. Be aware of the risk of powdery mildew and make sure to take action at any sign of it taking hold.

Ultimate Seeds

Indica-Dominant

Genetics: Sour Diesel x OG Kush x Amnesia Haze

Potency: THC 21%

ultimateseeds.com

The experience of smoking this strain has been likened to 'talking to God': a brave and bold claim, you might think. Parent plant Amnesia Haze is known to bring on a psychedelic, trippy high, and it could be this influence that leads the smoker into a state much like conversing with the ultimate deity. However we could also attribute this to the cerebral relaxation of the Sour Diesel, or the zombie-making super stone of OG Kush. Wherever it comes from, the high is a delightful one, leaving you positive, stimulated and chilled out all at the same time. The taste is layered and has both floral and oily undertones, and makes SDOGnesia a total joy to smoke.

Sensi Star

Paradise Seeds, one of the most notable Amsterdam seed companies, has released some fantastic original strains in the last decade or so, and one of these is their well-known Sensi Star. The family history of this plant is unknown, but it is an indica-dominant hybrid that has earned a great reputation since it was introduced to the market in 1995.

Having won many awards over the years, this diva has a lot to live up to. She does so by producing solid, dense colas that are extremely compact and drenched in frosty resin. A great plant to choose for an indoor grow, Sensi Star works particularly well in a SOG set up with 20 plants per square yard, potted closely together. Hydroponic and soil grows also suit her needs, though if you let her grow outside expect a huge plant of about 6.5 feet in height with very strong side branching. Indoors, you should let the vegetative stage run for 2 weeks before changing to a 12 on/12 off light cycle, and you'll be rewarded with very dark green fan leaves and weighty buds.

The citrusy-metallic scent of the nugs gives a fantastically dense smoke that devolves into a body-hitting stone that some note has added cerebral effects. Whether or not you feel the head high is more or less irrelevant, as you will be consumed with the body heaviness that makes Sensi Star a one-toke wonder.

Paradise Seeds, Holland

Indica-Dominant

Genetics: Unknown
Indica Hybrid

Potency: THC 15-18%

paradise-seeds.com

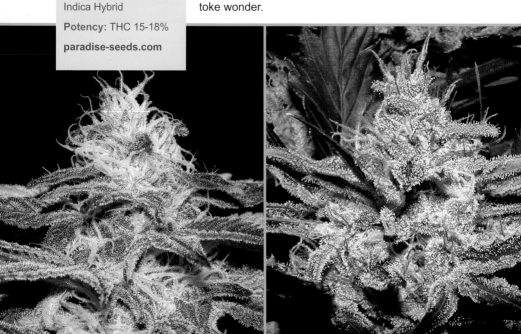

Shiesel

Bonguru Beans is a well-established Dutch seed company specializing in high quality niche genetics, such as their celebrated strain, Shiesel. By crossing a special cut of Shiva with a renowned New York City Diesel, the breeders at Bonguru Beans have created one hell of a plant. The Shiva adds a significant amount of potency to the NYC Diesel and the buds retain the floral bouquet with an extra hint of fruitiness from the Diesel parent. Shiesel is an F1 and subsequently shows the distinct differences of the parent strains in the phenotypes that are produced.

Growing this strain can be a challenge, both indoors and outdoors, but while beginners can find Shiesel to be a tough plant to grow, advanced cultivators enjoy the challenge and love this beauty because the rewards are so sweet. Flowering time is between 8 and 10 weeks with a decent yield if tended to properly. The breeder recommends that seeds be germinated by soaking overnight and then planted directly into small pots at a depth of ¼ inch. Be careful not to overwater and be sure to vegetate the plant until it has between 4 and 7 internodes.

Bonguru Beans, Holland

Indica-Dominant

Genetics: Shiva x New York City Diesel

Potency: THC 18%

bonguruseeds.com

Shiesel is a fruity, exotic-smelling plant with a firm, hashy taste. The stone is very indica-influenced, with some extreme couch lock. Chill out, put some tunes on, and get ready for a long relaxation session.

Sour Grapes

Having been growing cannabis since the early 90s, the breeders behind Apothecary Genetics have conducted years of research and development to create strains that are perfect for medical marijuana users like themselves. Sour Grapes is a cross made from two of Apothecary's own breeding strains, the celebrated Grape Ape, known for its fast finishing time and great taste, and the popular Sour Diesel, known for its great yields.

This strain is happy in any environment, but is not particularly suitable for a SOG technique. The plants enjoy having their own space and will reward you with an increased yield if you supply them with adequate feeding and sufficient space to grow. Sour Grapes is an even quicker plant than its Grape Ape parent, and should be fully finished in 7 or 8 weeks. If you're growing outside, be ready for harvest in late October.

Sour Grapes was created to be potent enough to help medical users while still tasting great, and every toke succeeds in this regard. A delicious and deep taste of wine grapes and sweet candy comes right before the soaring, euphoric body high that hits hard but doesn't result in couch lock, meaning that you can still go about your daily business easily enough. You'll just have a smile on your face while you do so.

Apothecary Genetics, USA

Indica-Dominant

Genetics: Grape Ape x Sour Diesel

Potency: THC 19-21%

apothecarygenetics.com

Starbud

Another small but serious young seed company based in the Netherlands, HortiLab uses primarily European and North American cannabis genetics to breed new-school strains, with the main goals of premium flavor, potency and yield. As yet they have four original breeds available, and of these four, two have won notable awards, indicating an up-and-coming company with a big future. One of these award-winners is their most prominent indica-heavy strain, StarBud, which was an underground legend in the US. The present-day StarBud is a clone from a private grower's seed line, coming from the U.S. midwest.

Named for its buds, so covered in resin that they "sparkle like stars", StarBud plants have an average indica stretch, and though indoors is the best situation for this plant, it can thrive well in outdoor grows in California and similar climates. However, high humidity should be avoided when grown inside, as the compact buds can give way to mold if the air is too wet. Be sure to keep the trim after harvest, as it can make great hash. StarBud seeds are fairly new to the market, so you might struggle to find grow reports to help you along with your crop. It will, however, make you as popular as that kid in the playground who has all the weird, limited-edition Pokémon stuff from Japan.

HortiLab Seed Company, Holland

Indica-Dominant

Genetics: Unknown

Midwest Strain

Potency: THC 14-20%

hortilab.nl

Still, you'll know if you're on the right track when you get a whiff of the sweet dankness that comes with the ripe buds, followed by the hashy taste of the smoke. Be ready for a heavy body stone with a pleasant head buzz. StarBud is a recent Cannabis Cup winner, and for good reason – this plant is fantastic!

Sweet Chunk

Switzerland's Alpine Seeds consistently impresses the community with its quality genetics and highly stabilized, niche strains. Sweet Chunk, a stunning cross of Sweet Pink Grapefruit and a Deep Chunk IBL, is no different. The indica dominance of this plant stems from its heritage, as Deep Chunk is a Pakistani/Aghani hybrid, and SPG is an old Northern Lights #1 phenotype. Breeders love this strain as it is not a poly-hybrid, and the Deep Chunk parent has dominated the cross, giving these plants perfectly homogenized and stabilized growth patterns.

These plants give hard and compact nuggets and a yield of around 30 to 40 grams each if grown to 32 inches. Sweet Chunk clones take just 10 days to root, so if you find one you like, it's easy to keep her as a mother plant. Plants are mold and spider mite resistant, but be sure to use a minimum of 2 to 4 weeks of light at 18 on/6 off to ensure healthy growth. This plant is not compatible with maxi-cropping or any cutting of the stalk prior to harvest.

Alpine Seeds, Switzerland

Indica-Dominant

Genetics: Sweet Pink Grapefruit x Deep Chunk IBL

Potency: THC 16-20%

alpine-seeds.ch

Expect a munchies-inducing couch lock to hit you hard and fast, but this is offset by the mild uplifting buzz that sets in after a little while. The SPG heritage means that Sweet Chunk tastes and smells of grapefruit, with sweet and fruity undertones and a hashy aftertaste.

Tahoe Gold

Master Thai Seeds is a solid independent breeder from North America, and has over 35 years experience growing with organics. Tahoe Gold is one of his best strains. A 50/50 indica/sativa strain, this has the genes of a real 1968 Skunk #1 straight from the breeders of Cali which was bred with a Hindu Kush grown from seed, circa 1975.

A versatile plant which can adapt well to any grow method, this plant is like the tortoise rather than the hare; it starts off slowly but before you know it, it'll be growing full steam ahead and surpassing other strains at the end of the flowering stage. Tahoe Gold tends to spread its branches out around a large central bud, staying fairly short throughout its whole life, and for this reason, is a good choice if you're working with a SOG set up. Finishing times range from 62 days indoors, through 65 days in a greenhouse, to a full 72-day cycle if you place them outside, with a harvest in October. Expect to yield around 100 grams per plant if you're growing indoors with 1000 watts of light.

Grown for the medicinal user, Tahoe Gold relaxes the body and prompts a positive state of mind while leaving the smoker still able to function. Remember though that, like all strains, it hits much harder if cooked into edibles. Carrying a sweet taste and a great buzz, this strain is one that is both enjoyable and effective.

Master Thai Seeds, USA

Indica-Dominant

Genetics: 1968 Skunk #1 x 1975 Hindu Kush

Potency: THC 17%

masterthai.com

Taiga

Holland's Dutch Passion have been big players in the scene since their inception in 1987, and now stand as one of the oldest and most well-known seed companies. Taiga, along with Tundra, was one of the first Dutch Passion auto-flowering strains released to the market in early 2009, and their success and popularity led the company to develop their new AutoFem strain line. The ruderalis line which gives this range its auto-flowering trait can all be traced back to plants obtained from the Northern latitudes in Russia and Canada. To create Taiga, the breeders at Dutch Passion took the pollen from an extremely early-flowering male Power Plant and fertilized the female ruderalis/indica cross.

With usual ruderalis resilience, Taiga does not ask for a special fertilizing regime, which means that it's easy to grow and can thrive almost anywhere. As the plants never grow huge, with a maximum height of about 24 inches, containers of 1.5 to 2 liters are sufficient to guarantee a good harvest, but for a good quality yield, the plants will need a place with a lot of sunlight. If given this, she will reward you with big, compact buds in less than 10 weeks. Under artificial light, 18 hours of light during 2 to 2.5 months is fine to ensure a decent harvest. As neither the fertilizing nor the light cycles need a lot of attention, with Taiga you can dedicate yourself to ensuring that she has plenty of grow space under your bulbs, that each flowering part of the plant has access to that light, and that no pests or diseases even have a chance of taking hold. Ladybugs, spider mites and aphids can all create problems that quickly become serious and can effectively kill half your crop. The dreaded botrytis is probably the main disease to look out for, as this grey mold loves humid rooms that are lacking in good ventilation. The only way to treat this is to remove every single part of the plant that has been touched by it, meaning that your vigorous, bushy plant can quickly end up as a spindly, pathetic wreck. With the correct protection and action against these problems, however, you should find Taiga a hassle-free strain to grow, and one that's particularly great if you're new to growing your own pot or are an industrial grower without a lot of time to tend to each individual plant in your massive garden.

Dutch Passion, Holland

Indica-Dominant

Genetics: Auto-flowering Ruderalis/Indica x Power Plant

dutch-passion.nl

Taiga buds carry a soft smoke with a cozy body stone and a very pleasant emotional warmth, but won't put you out for too long. The smoke is very reminiscent of Power Plant, with a sharp taste.

Taleggio

America's Alphakronik Genes already has some fantastic strains to its name and this brand new indica-dominant plant won't let down its already stellar reputation. Released to the public on St Patrick's day in 2011, Taleggio is named after a particularly pungent and fruity type of Italian cheese in order to give a cheeky nod to its Exodus Cheese parent plant. Exodus Cheese is a UK strain known for its strong, creeping high, and is paired with the phenomenal Space Queen in this great new strain.

Taleggio is said to surpass even the most aromatic of Cheese strains, so odor control must be your biggest priority when growing this lady, especially when she enters the flowering stage. There are a couple of phenotypes that vary slightly, but Taleggio plants will not have much stretch, being predominantly short and bushy. Finishing in 55 to 65 days, she's a medium yielder, but with Taleggio it's is all about taste and potency.

Prepare yourself for a deliciously overwhelming attack on the taste buds when you light up a Taleggio bowl! An abundance of flavors from blueberry and vanilla to strawberries and cream will ease you into the super strong high, and the couch lock is the only thing that will stop you from finishing the rest of your stash – and only because you can't reach it.

Alphakronik Genes, USA

Indica-Dominant

Genetics: Exodus Cheese x Space Queen

cannabis-seeds-bank.co.uk

tksauctions.net

rollitup.org

Taskenti

CannaBioGen is a very well-respected cannabis collective that currently operates out of Spain. The team is serious about its work and has a well-deserved and excellent reputation for reliable genetics. Taking a more scientific approach to cannabis research and development they have several incredible original strains that are popular with connoisseur growers, breeders and tokers. Taskenti is a pure indica that originated in Uzbekistan, but CannaBioGen worked hard to stabilize the most valuable traits of the plant to make it suitable for a variety of grow situations in the Western world.

This strain tends to vegetate quickly and looks like your archetypal indica plant. With heavy branching, very deep green leaves and big, fat buds, it is the bulldog of the growing world and is certainly not to be messed with, taking to soil particularly well and scaring off pests before they get their nasty little teeth into it. However, a little tenderness also goes a long way, and aeroponic systems allow Taskenti to bloom beautifully. This strain flowers without too much effort, and is a good plant if you're

CannaBioGen, Spain

Pure Indica

Genetics: Uzbekistani

cannabiogen.com

planning on an early harvest as it doesn't need the extra couple of weeks for flowering that some strains prefer. The vegetative stage should last for a bare minimum of 30 days, with plants maturing fully in 7 to 9 weeks. Ensure that the atmosphere in your grow room is well-ventilated and dry, particularly during the flowering period.

For an even greater yield you can grow Taskenti outdoors and it is especially well-suited to climates similar to those of the mountains of southern Spain. If so, plan to harvest in October. Always a good choice for a novice grower, Taskenti can withstand many typical newbie mistakes.

Your resulting Taskenti bud will be noticeably heavier than many other types and does not have the overpowering stench that you might expect. A little trimming will be necessary, as these nugs often contain more leaves than other strains, but putting in a little effort to beautify your bud will definitely be worthwhile. The tight buds will burn quickly and smoothly if cured properly, which is a pleasure to see. The thick smoke is a bit of a cougher, but gives you a nice full feeling giving way to a serious but mellow high that leaves you with no hangover the next day. It does taste good, and as you'll feel amazing the in the morning too it's very tempting to hit the pipe again the next day with more and more, but try to pace yourself in working through your stash, as you'll find yourself dozing if you go over the top.

The Happy Brother BX2

Karma Genetics are British breeders operating from Maastricht in the Netherlands. The tale goes that this strain originates from a private grower, a Rasta from Amsterdam, who was growing to medicate his paralyzed brother. Karma got a hold of some clones in the late 90s, worked hard with several other plants, struggling to get a stable offspring, until ChemDawg came through to produce The Happy Brother BX2.

The Happy Brother BX2 is known to produce decent buds under even a small amount of light, Just 400 watts can stimulate enough growth to please any grower, breeder or smoker. It won't be a large yielder, but the buds you do get will be hefty, and don't shrink when dried. Your crop will be stocky, with thick branching and wide leaves, making it unnecessary to give plants any additional support in the flowering stage. They should finish anywhere between 9 and 11 weeks, depending on your lighting cycles or the climate.

Karma says that this strain is all about the taste, and he's right; the smoke is smooth and the taste is multi-layered, with citrusy fruit giving way to a musky, dank, skunk-like sensation. Expect a cerebral, psychoactive high moving down through the body in a relaxing sweep.

Karma Genetics, Holland

Indica-Dominant

Genetics: Happy Brother x Happy Brother BX1

Potency: THC 17%

karmagenetics.com

TNT Kush

Eva Female Seeds is a Spanish seed company with a variety of excellent strains that are popular throughout Europe and the rest of the world. TNT Kush is a well-respected variety that was carefully selected from seeds brought to Spain from the mountains of Pakistan. TNT Kush is a landrace Pakistani, and has been carefully backcrossed for years in order to create a highly reliable and potent strain.

If you get your hands on some TNT Kush seeds, you'll be pleased to see that, like all Pakistani indicas, she produces large numbers of trichomes and hard, compact buds. Though this is a great sight for any grower, it does means that you need to stake your plants carefully, and avoid touching the buds too much before harvest. TNT Kush is very easy to grow, especially in nitrogen-poor soils, and requires very few nutrients to thrive. The plant flowers in 55 to 60 days, indoors and out. Expect long shoots during outdoor grows. Indoor growers should keep the temperature high during flowering to promote bigger, more resinous buds.

Eva Female Seeds, Spain

Pure Indica

Genetics: Pakistani Kush

Potency: THC 19-21%

evaseeds.com

Expect a nutty smell with hints of fruit and cypress evergreen undertones. The taste is very rich, with hints of bitter almond and even chocolate. Due to the high THC content, TNT Kush bud is very strong smoke. Get some treats ready in advance, and have fun!

Tony's Superfrosty

California's Redstar Farms is a collective dedicated to producing strains that ease the PTSD and trauma of disabled veterans and medical users. Tony's Superfrosty is an original strain born of Blackberry Kush, 98 Bubba Kush and Afghan lineage, and as such is a strong indica-dominant variety with heavy Kush features and the type of stone that will give respite to those it's intended for. Bubba Kush in particular is considered by many to be one of the best current strains, and adding Blackberry and Afghani genetics to the mix means that this is one serious strain.

Tony's Superfrosty grows well in both soil and hydroponic set ups, and can be happily cultivated indoors or out. You can expect a finishing time of around 9 weeks, with a significant yield. Due to the strong indica influence, these plants will be short and strong, with extremely sturdy branches. They respond well to topping and are very forgiving to any mistakes you might make.

The quality of the amazingly resinous nugs you harvest will make up for a yield that is smaller than that of others indicas. The sweet taste, smooth smoke and the heavy, therapeutic narcotic feeling it gives will send you straight back to your grow room to plant some more seeds – once you've had a nap, of course.

Redstar Farms, USA

Indica-Dominant

Genetics: Blackberry Kush x 98 Bubba x Afghan

Potency: THC 18%

redstar420.com

Towerful

Spain's Tropical Seeds Company has taken advantage of their subtropical location and amazing climate to grow and breed all year round, allowing for huge leaps forward in the few years that the company has been in business. To create Towerful, they've used their own pure sativa Congo Pointe Noir, a company favorite, and a Chitral Kush from Pakistan, resulting in a pretty spectacular indica-dominant hybrid.

Despite such fantastic sativa genetics, Towerful grows like a pure indica – exhibiting strong stems and branches with dark, wide leaves. Its tendency to form just one solid top cola makes it ideal for high-density indoor grows. The flowering period of this strain lies between 60 and 65 days, during which time you'll see big white buds appear, with a high calyx-to-leaf ratio that will leave you itching to harvest! In time, purple shades will also come through, along with woody aromas of hash. While your bud will smell good enough to smoke right after it's dried, a longer curing process will only enhance the fragrance, taste and potency of Towerful, so leave it as long as you can!

Tropical Seeds Company, Spain

Indica-Dominant

Genetics: Congo Pointe Noir x Pakistan Chitral Kush

Potency: THC 19%

tropicalseedscompany.com

This strain is a very quick hitter, and even while you're enjoying the earthy smoke and trying to place that taste – it's a hint of wine – the lively, giggly high will grab you and refuse to let go. This gives way to a narcotic effect as time passes, and you'll be amazingly relaxed.

Whitaker Blues

JD Short, son of the famous DJ Short's, has done his family proud with this fantastic indica-dominant strain. This is a true Oregon heritage cross that connoisseurs and new tokers alike will adore. The mother of Whitaker Blues is a plant referred to as "Quimby" – an old-school, West Coast cut that is reminiscent of a classic, early indica lineage with a strong, sleepy effect on the smoker. The Quimby mother was crossed with DJ Short's personally selected Blueberry father, making Whitaker Blues 80% indica and 20% sativa in structure.

Whitaker Blues is a stout hybrid with short branching structures and large, compact buds that are loaded with resin. Be sure to check the buds for mold, as their density can give rise to the warmth that mold loves. Growers like this plant's vigor, productivity, and fantastic violet and blue coloration. This plant finishes in 55 to 62 days and can be grown indoors or outdoors as in Sarah's accompanying photographs.

Finished buds have a pungent/sweet velvety grape flavor with undertones of vanilla. The high from this bud, whether you're smoking or consuming it in edibles, is pleasantly strong with a slight initial buzz that causes increased appetite and a very relaxed and calm experience.

JD Short of DJ Short Seeds, Canada

Indica-Dominant

Genetics: Thai x Oaxaca x Afghani

Potency: THC 17%

legendsseeds.com

greatcanadianseeds.com

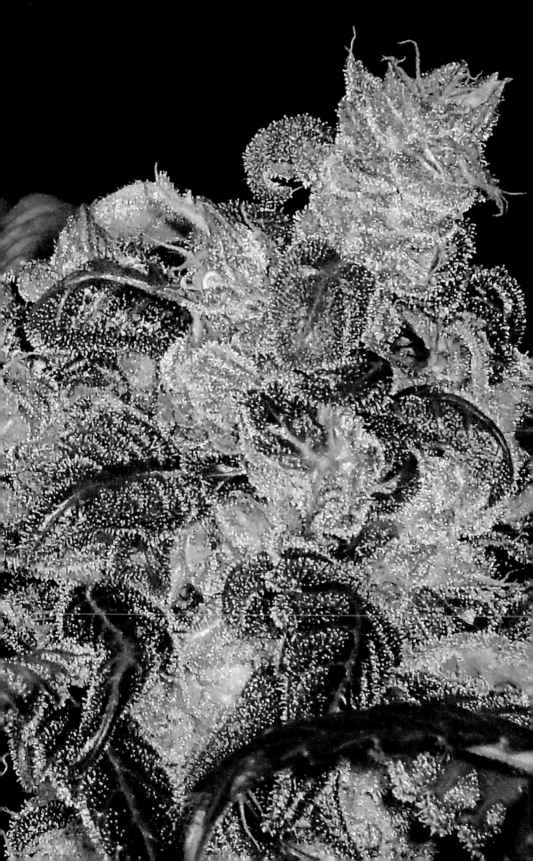

White Russian

White Russian from Holland's Serious Seeds is an indica-dominant plant with some impressive parental genetics. White Russian is a stable cross of AK-47 and a prize-winning White Widow clone. Because of the AK-47 genetics, White Russian contains Colombian, Mexican, Thai and Afghani genetics, making its background remarkably vibrant and consistently reliable. The quality, consistency and potency of both AK-47 and White Widow have been maintained in this plant, making it a fantastic addition to any garden.

White Russian grows to a medium height and produces consistent, dense and resinous flower tops with crystals appearing after about five weeks of flowering. Be sure to have a good air filtration system as the plants are strong smelling during both their vegetative and flowering period. This is known as one of the most potent strains available, so be careful that you don't get a contact high from the highly resinous buds.

The high is strong, long lasting and is quite cerebral due to the AK-47's sativa influences. White Russian is a great medicinal plant with excellent attributes from both of its parent plants, including a smooth taste and strong high. This plant has great bag appeal because of its super pungent aroma and consistent bud shape and texture. Bear in mind that AK-47 is known as a 'one hit wonder' strain, meaning that even a single toke can put you out.

Serious Seeds, Holland

Indica-Dominant

Genetics: AK-47 x White Widow

Potency: THC 22%

seriousseeds.com

X-18 Pure Pakistani

Working out of the USA, Reserva Privada is a collective of West Coast breeders that strives to fashion fantastic and innovative strains for use in the community. Although protected by medical growing laws in their home state, these breeders prefer to remain nameless. One of their great strains is a pure indica with Pakistani landrace genetics known as X-18 Pure Pakistani. This is testament to the workability of the true Pakistani line, and the quality of X-18 proves the strength of true Hindu Kush plants.

Though this plant is an indica through and through, the landrace influence means that its growing pattern may be much different than you're used to with indica/sativa hybrids. You'll definitely spot the fat, intensely green leaves to which you've become accustomed as an indica grower but once you reach the first few weeks of the flowering stage, you'll see the typical Pakistani stretch that makes your plants look much different. With steady growth throughout its lifespan, this isn't a particularly fast-flowering plant but it should be fully finished in 8 to 9 weeks. In flower, its aroma becomes especially pungent and when you get a whiff of the cheese and chorizo smell you'll be looking around for your roommate's leftover pizza, and might get a shock to find that that strangely delicious odor is actually emanating from your plants. This might also be an asset in the security of your crop, as no one in their right mind would associate weed growing with a meaty smell. Towards the end of flowering, however, your plants will take on a more vinegary, citric smell, and that's when you'll have to be extra careful to ventilate and extract the odor properly.

Reserva Privada, USA

Pure Indica

Genetics: Pakistani

Indica

dnagenetics.com

Your harvest from X-18 Pure Pakistani won't be huge, but you will walk away with a decent stash of rock-hard, crusty, compact nugs that reek of quality. For each square yard of grow room indoors, you will most likely take away about 400 to 500 grams of dried, cured bud. These buds will be very easy to manicure as the calyx-to-leaf ratio is so high, and they'll be literally crusted with that beautiful resin; just be sure not to touch your eyes before washing your hands.

The high point of growing this strain is when you finally get to roll your homegrown X-18 Pure Pakistani joint, and as you inhale the citrusy, acidy smoke that slides down your windpipe you'll see why this is revered as such a fantastic strain. Then comes the head rush and the spinning feeling, and your personality and situation will decide what comes next: whether it's the relaxing sleepiness or the brainstorming energy, be sure to enjoy it to its full potential.

PHOTOS BY RANDOM00

Zombie Rasta

With a myriad of brilliantly-named cannabis strains out there you have to pull something very special out of the bag to make an impression on jaded tokers, and Spain's Hero Seeds have definitely done that with Zombie Rasta. This name is a clever play on the name of one of its parent strains, Marley's Collie, which was named after the legendary dead reggae star Bob Marley – 'collie' being slang for weed in his native Jamaica. This Jamaican and Afghani indica mix by was crossed with another indica, Black Domina, which is a blend of Afghani, Canadian Ortega, Northern Lights and Hash Plant.

   With such a rich gene pool, Zombie Rasta plants are something special. Owing to the strong influence of Marley's Collie, these crops have wide, hefty leaves of the deepest green and a massive central cola if left untopped, which they prefer. Thanks to their good but not overly-extensive spread, they work well in a SOG set up as well as regular indoor soil grows. For the best harvest possible, be sure to give the right mix of nutrients and enough feeding. Zombie Rasta is more suited to indoor and greenhouse grows, in which you can expect flowering in 60 days and plant heights of up to 65 inches.

Hero Seeds, Spain

Indica-Dominant

Genetics: Black Domina (Afghan) x Bob Marley Collie

Potency: THC 23-26%

heroseeds.com

The sativa influence, which comes from Marley's Collie, also brings a very heady feel to the physical high and the combination of these two will leave you feeling mellow and chilled. The taste is fruity yet sour at the same time, like those little neon candies that fizzle on your tongue, yet a bit more mature.

Zombie Virus

OGA Seeds is a Canadian seed bank offering high quality, unique strains for growers around the world. For their fabulously-named Zombie Virus, they have crossed their two favorite strains from 2008: a beautiful pure indica mom and a Diesel cross dad. The stability of the mother plant and the grapey undertones of the father give a plant that is a joy to both grow and smoke, no matter what your toke tolerance.

The ease of growing Zombie Virus makes it a good choice for growers of any level, and it also clones easily, too. With its mother's durable form, this plant can handle a lot of nutrients and responds well to fertilizer, but if you're working with an outdoor grow, you should ensure that it doesn't get rained on too much due to its sticky nature. It responds well to topping, but continues a steady growth even without. Even in a 3 gallon pot, Zombie Virus will give a substantial yield. Don't leave it in the vegetative stage for too long, especially if growing indoors, as it will become unruly. If you have room for the 8 feet tall plants outside, then let them go mad.

OGA Seeds, Canada

Indica-Dominant

Genetics: Pure Indica x Diesel

Potency: THC 19%

ogas.ca

If its ability to grow almost on its own gives it the Virus tag, then the stone definitely gives rise to the Zombie part of the name: stoners smoking this strain will be put into a living dead stupor by the oily, grapey buds no matter what their smoking habits are. Get infected!

Index

Index

Index

Index